Hamm

Narvi

Trondheim

Archangel

erodvinsk
(Molotovsk)

Helsinki

• Leningrad

*Stockholm

S O V I E T   U N I O N

* Moscow

*Copenhagen

* Berlin

Warsaw *

Map drawn by Maria Campbell Brent.

Escape from Archangel
An American Merchant Seaman at War

By Thomas E. Simmons

During World War II, merchant marine tankers in convoys plied the frozen North Atlantic through the flaming wreckage of torpedoed ships. Working to keep sea lanes open, valiant merchant seamen supplied food, fuel, and goods to the Allies in the last pockets of European resistance to the Nazis.

This exciting book acknowledges that the merchant marines, all volunteers, are among the unsung heroes of the war. One of these was Jac Smith, an ordinary seaman on the *Cedar Creek*, a new civilian tanker lend-leased to the U.S.S.R. and in the merchantman convoy running from Scotland to Murmansk. Smith's riveting adventures at sea and in the frozen taigas and tundra are a story of valor that underlines the essential role of merchant marines in the war against the Axis powers.

This gripping narrative tells of a cruel blow that fate dealt Smith when, after volunteering to serve on the tanker headed for Murmansk, he was arrested and interned in a Soviet work camp near Arkhangelsk.

Escape from Archangel recounts how this American happened to be imprisoned in an Allied country and how he planned and managed his escape. In his arduous 900-mile trek to freedom he encountered the remarkable Laplanders of the far north and brave Norwegian resistance fighters. While telling this astonishing story of Jac Smith and of the awesome dangers merchant seamen endured while keeping commerce alive on the seascape of war, *Escape from Archangel* brings long deserved attention to the role of the merchant marines and their sacrifices during wartime.

Continued on back flap

U.S. Merchant Marine recruiting poster, World War II

ESCAPE

FROM

ARCHANGEL

An American Merchant Seaman at War

by

THOMAS E. SIMMONS

UNIVERSITY PRESS OF MISSISSIPPI
Jackson & London

93 92 91 90   4 3 2 1
The paper in this book meets the guidelines for
permanence and durability of the Committee on Production
Guidelines for Book Longevity of the Council on
Library Resources.

Library of Congress Cataloging-in-Publication Data

Simmons, Thomas E., 1936–
     Escape from Archangel : an American merchant seaman at
war / by Thomas E. Simmons.
          p.   cm.
     ISBN 0–87805–461–8
     1. Smith, O. M. 2. Merchant marine—United States—Biogra-
phy.
     3. Prisoners of war—Soviet Union—Biography. 4. Escapes—
Russian S.F.S.R.—Siberia—History—20th century. 5. Siberia
(R.S.F.S.R.)—
     History.   I. Title.
     D810.T8S48   1990
     957.08'092—dc20
     [B]   90–38401
                                                                CIP

British Library Cataloging-in-Publication data available

Contents

Preface

The following story is true. It was told to the author by O. M. (Jac) Smith, Jr., retired merchant seaman, (Merchant Marine Combat Bar, Atlantic War Zone Bar, Pacific War Zone Bar, Korean Service Bar, Vietnam Service Bar), during interviews conducted from August 1988 through August 1989 at his home in Biloxi, Mississippi. A man of quiet dignity, he had—out of modesty, out of painful memories—put away for more than forty years the remarkable story you are about to read. The events taken from Mr. Smith's own carefully chosen words and the facts presented from months of research will transport you through World War II convoy duty in the North Atlantic on the infamous Murmansk Run to an impossible escape to freedom from a frozen hell where no American had gone before.

The author worked in association with shippers, carriers, and ports for more than seven years, and was a member of the National Maritime Council prior to its sad demise. It is his hope that this true story will help to renew an appreciation of the American merchant seaman of World War II.

No author's finished work stands as his alone. The idea, the concept, the written words, the style are, more or less, his. But the finished book—tidy, free of awkward structure, grammatical errors, lapses in syntax, all the things that make a book easier for the reader—are primarily brought about by the unsung editors; I hereby sing the praises of two such heros. My deepest thanks to senior editor, JoAnne Prichard, University Press of Mississippi, and to copy editor, Ann Finlayson, veteran of New York's publishing world.

I owe a debt of thanks to US Navy Rear Admiral Kemp Tolley (Ret.), naval historian, whose knowledge and dedication to accurate detail, proved invaluable.

Many thanks to the research personnel of the libraries of Mississippi's universities and colleges, and those of Harrison County's library system.

Credit is given elsewhere for those organizations, individuals, and institutions who provided the photographs used in this book. I thank them.

I especially thank Frank O. Braynard, Curator, American Merchant Marine Museum Foundation, Kings Point, New York, for his enthusiasm, encouragement, and aid.

To Larry Molony, gentleman, friend, bandy-legged captain of the *Last Resort*, (aboard which we have shared more than a few adventures), I give appreciation for his time spent reading the manuscript and providing valued suggestions.

Last, I thank O. M. (Jac) Smith for the courage and pain it took to unlock the closet in his mind where he had put away his remarkable story for more than forty-five years.

To the men who served and were quietly forgotten.

They were professional seamen in the American Merchant Marine. The public sometimes confused them with the Navy, sometimes with the Marines. Others called them feather merchants or draft dodgers. After the war the government refused to grant them veterans' benefits. Yet the American Merchant Marine suffered catastrophic losses during World War II—proportionally greater losses than those of all American armed forces except (by 0.1 of 1 percent) the U.S. Marine Corps. The total number of Allied merchant ships sunk between August 1939 and the war's end on August 15, 1945, total in the thousands; 948 of them were American. The number of Allied merchant seamen who gave their lives has been estimated at over 40,000, and 6,000 of those were Americans. Britain lost 32,000, almost one out of every three men who served.

This book is dedicated to every one of them,
heroes of the sea.

Prologue: Just an
Old Bridgetender?

Quietly a man came home from the sea, from more than thirty years at sea. He had sailed across all the oceans, past all the islands, round all the continents of earth. Home to Biloxi, Mississippi. Home because he grew up there. Home to care for his aging mother. Home.

He found Biloxi relatively unchanged from his last visit. There were fewer of the stately old hotels, true, displaced by the so-called progress of sprawling motels. There was a new building or two here and there, and the tawdry beach strip now sported everything from all-girl revues to putt-putt golf. The fishing fleet was still there, but the old sailing schooners which used to crowd the Back Bay were gone. The old canneries had dwindled away one by one; no longer did the loud long whine of their whistles awake the cannery workers,—French, Slavs, Danes, Austrians, and Bohemians, the school-mates he had grown up with—to a long day of backbreaking work. Their children now owned fishing boats or shops, or had become the professional citizens of Biloxi.

But, all in all, Biloxi hadn't changed much. He was not so much a stranger to the place as he was to himself—a stranger to the boy he had been when he left home late in 1942. So long ago.

In appearance the man looked weathered from years spent aboard ship. He had laid telegraph cable across the Atlantic, worked on a whaling ship, fished off the Grand Banks, and served in the Merchant Marine during three wars. His skin had been toughened by the wind, sea, and salt. His hair, an undefined color somewhere between light blond and silver gray, was no longer the flaming red of his childhood. His eyes were still bright blue, if dimmed a little by uncountable hours spent scanning endless horizons, and he was still tall and thin. But he was older than his years. As a young man he had had to deal with that certain kind of rapid mental and physical aging thrust upon some by uncommon adventure. He still had his health, except when it got cold. He didn't like the cold. He would never forget the cold.

He could not simply retire, at least not at first. More than thirty years of being constantly on the go had molded a pattern which he could not easily break. He would have to ease himself into retirement. First work on being home, then on being retired.

After a few months he was offered a job as tender on the old bridge across Back Bay. Some might not have wanted it, but his grandfather and his father had been bridgetenders after their retirements. For Jac it was the perfect job. He was on the water, and he had time to fish, to think, to sort out his life. It was easy to come to Biloxi physically; the time he spent on the bridge would help him to come home in his mind.

He was no stranger to the old Back Bay bridge—the two-lane concrete ribbon set on aging wooden pilings, its 1920s lamppost rusting, most of the once-graceful lamp globes broken by vandals or storms. So what if it was slated for replacement? He liked the solitude of the bridge and the beauty of Back Bay: noon bright or moonlight, the dark waters ever changing reflections of shoreline and cloud.

He ignored the automobiles that zoomed across, uncaring, but he waved genially to the boaters, shrimpers, oystermen, fishermen, sailors, and water skiers of Back Bay, and they usually had time to return the waves and occasionally to exchange spoken greetings. There is a tradition of courtesy common to those who travel by water; it comes about from the necessity of depending upon others, often strangers, for survival, from the respect for one's fellows learned by those who have seen the tricks of the sea.

Recreational boating was the rage, he found, but many of the new sailors who went down to the bay in plastic boats lacked a knowledge of seamanship and a sense of the traditional courtesy of the sea. Jac was not very tolerant of poor seamanship.

One day, a speedboat full of careless young revelers forced a shrimper to ram the bridge fenders, in order to avoid hitting a fallen water skier. Jac let them know what he thought of their recklessness. And a lifetime at sea had given him a colorful vocabulary to draw upon when he needed it.

One of the skiers wanted to take issue with Jac, but the skipper, one hand holding a beer, the other arm draped around a shapely young bikini-clad lovely, said, "Ah! To hell

with him. He's just an old fart of a bridgetender." He let go of
the girl and opened the throttle, leaving the derisive laughter
of the group echoing among the bridge pilings.

"Just an old bridgetender, huh?" Jac said to himself. He
watched the boat disappear rapidly down the bay toward
Point Cadet. He was angry at the rudeness, angry at ignorance
and what he perceived to be the abuse of the privilege of
freedom. Then he thought, What the hell. Maybe I still take
things too seriously. Aboard ship I'd have straightened out
those kids with a marlinspike, a splicing fid, or my fists. Well,
times change. Maybe I *have* become an old fart.

He thought about it as he watched the sun slide blazing
behind a broad pink layer of cloud. Then he leaned on the
bridge railing and stared down into the dark water.

"I don't remember being like those kids," he said aloud.
"Maybe we never had the time. We sure never had the money.
Just a bridgetender, eh?"

The tide was falling, swirling around the bridge pilings,
running out of Bayou Bernard, out of the Biloxi River, down
from the Tchoutacabouffa River, toward the inlet between
Ocean Springs and Biloxi, and out into the Gulf of Mexico.
He looked across the Back Bay where the north end of his
bridge met the shore. When his grandmother had lived on
that shore, the bridge had been a one-lane wooden structure,
a toll bridge that cost two cents to walk across, seven cents
for a mule and wagon, and ten cents for an automobile. By
the late twenties the county had scraped up enough money
to build a new two-lane replacement of concrete, the bridge
Jac now tended.

"Now *it* needs to be replaced," he mused. His father had
flame-heated and bent by hand most of the steel that was

reinforcing the concrete in the bridge. It had been hard work, but it had fed the family when jobs were scarce. That was long before the war, before the convoys crossed the North Atlantic, before the cold.

For a moment, as he gazed down the long and deserted bridge through the dimming light, he thought he could see a group of schoolchildren walking toward him, barefoot and laughing. And then he realized the children were walking in his mind, that their laughter was an echo across time—that he was one of them.

Drifting there, in the timeless reaches of his mind, he remembered.

Biloxi, 1936

O. M. Smith, Jr., answers to "Jac." He never liked the names his initials stood for—you called him Oswald Marion at your own risk—and early on he let it be known that he would be called Jac, without a *k.* He was tall and thin and had fire-red hair. A quiet young man, he could be stubborn at times, and he wasn't much for putting up with foolishness—unless, of course, he was the one being foolish, which he often was. He was a good son, a dependable friend, a not-so-good student, a musician of sorts, a better sailor, a not bad fisherman. He didn't mind work and never set out to start trouble, although he didn't walk away from it either—there were boney-hard fists at the ends of those long arms. It was the whipping he got when he arrived home with "skint knuckles" that taught him to use diplomacy in a crisis.

His grandmother was determined his hands would be fit for playing the piano. Never mind the hard times. Her grandchildren would be "raised right," a Southern term that meant children would be handled with dignity, discipline, true Southern culture, a sense of heritage, a fair measure of religion—all reinforced by the use of a firm hand.

Jac's sister Elizabeth was born in Louisiana, but Jac was born in Tishomingo County, northern Mississippi, where his father worked for a lumber company until it went broke in the Great Depression. For a while the family tried to make do picking cotton. Jac remembers following his mother, pulling the cotton and putting it in a huge sack. His mother made him a smaller sack. He would follow her down the rows of knee-high cotton sprouting from Tishomingo County gravel. Sometimes he fell asleep between the cotton rows, resting his head on the cotton he had picked. Eventually the family had no choice but to return home to the Gulf Coast, where his grandmother had a small farm in D'Iberville, across Back Bay from Biloxi. They grew all the vegetables and fruit they needed, and fish, shrimp, and crabs were abundant in the bay. They slept on mattresses stuffed with corn shucks and carded raw wool for quilts. His grandmother received butter, milk, and eggs as payment for music lessons. His father worked at whatever he could find. Things like shoes and new clothes were harder to come by, but the Smiths were no worse off than most families at the time.

At night, Jac and his sister would sit on the floor while their mother taught them geography. First the states and all their capitals, then the countries and capitals around the world. Jac dreamed of one day seeing all these marvelous places his mother taught them about on those evenings by the light of kerosene lamps. At school he would tell his classmates that he would one day travel the world. They thought he was crazy.

It was by kerosene lamps, one on each side of the keyboard, that his grandmother, Hattie Seale, began the musical education of the children. This meant endless hours of piano training. "If you missed a note," Jac says, "you got your knuckles cracked with a ruler. If you played the right notes, you got praise and a gold star. Grandmother taught music along the coast for fifty-eight years, and many a musician remembers the cracked knuckles given by Mrs. Seale. I have enjoyed the piano all my life."

Jac's childhood revolved around education, chores, odd jobs, and boats. There were plenty of boats on Back Bay, where fishing wasn't for fun, it was for food.

It was not his family that was poor. South Mississippi was poor. Almost every family in the region had been hit hard by the Great Depression. This did not mean people lacked education and culture. The South has always prided itself on being genteel, and Mississippians were no strangers to hardship. The Civil War had broken them, Reconstruction crippled them, and just as the good times of the 1920s had finally filtered down to the Gulf Coast, the Depression rolled in, busting a real estate and building boom and bankrupting a string of brand new resort hotels, not to mention a few banks.

But the Gulf Coast was a better place than most in which to grow up during the Depression. If there weren't many jobs, there was good fishing and crabbing. Many a family was fed by the generous Gulf—so much so that mullet became widely known as Biloxi Bacon. Nearly every house in Biloxi had a cast net hanging from a tree limb ready for the next mullet run. Along with hardship, there was love and family, school and books, friendship and dreams of better times. And there was unshakable faith in old-time Southern religion.

Jac's great-great-uncle built the first cabin at the Methodist Seashore Camp Grounds. There families congregated each year for a much-anticipated occasion, social in nature as well as religious—two to three weeks under the great moss-covered oaks cooled by fresh breezes from the Gulf. Young and old enjoyed the holiday equally. At the Camp Grounds, one could hear the laughter of young children at play, the giggling chatter of young ladies throwing glances at clusters of young men trying to look disinterested. Many a first kiss was experienced in the summer moonlight, in spite of the strict attendance rules for meetings and early curfews. The center of activity and news was the kitchen hall, where wives and mothers gathered to prepare picnic-style meals and exchange the latest gossip. Other groups met around Four Armed Charlie, an artesian well with four outlets that furnished clear, ice cold water.

In the fall there was school. Children who lived in Biloxi had a short mile or two walk to Howard No. 1 School, but the Smith children and others who lived across Back Bay in D'Iberville walked barefoot across the bridge to Howard School in Biloxi. 1936 was the year that much of Back Bay froze, an unheard-of phenomenon. The children, still without school shoes, had to run across the long ice-covered bridge to keep their feet from sticking to the frozen surface. On the far side, they scraped the ice off the soles of their feet on the ever-present mounds of oyster shells at the seafood factory near the south end of the bridge. Their feet were as tough as horsehide.

The children did not complain much. They went to school, they helped at home, they laughed easily, they played when they could, and they prepared their lessons every night. They were tough in a nice way. They got on with what they had, which builds character. It was the character and the courage of their generation that would later maintain freedom in the world when the struggling masses of Europe allowed a frustrated little Austrian artist named Hitler to plunge the world once more into war.

Mama, I'm Going to Sea

The European war remained far off at first, something exciting you heard on the radio or read about in newspapers. But it brought unexpected economic expansion to the farms and factories. Ingalls Ship Yard in nearby Pascagoula suddenly came out of the depression doldrums as steamship lines placed orders for new vessels, and clangs and bustle filled the once silent ways. Jac's father and the fathers of his generation got better work, and there was a little more money. The Smith family moved to a house in Biloxi near the railroad station. It had electricity.

This was long before America's entry into the war, but U.S. merchant seamen were already dying in the North Atlantic. President Roosevelt had managed to induce Congress to pass the Lend-Lease bill, under which arms, munitions, and other war material was "lent" to the Allies, whose resolute resistance to Hitler was keeping war away from our shores. "We must be the arsenal of Democracy," he told the nation in late

1940. All these goods had to be shipped across seas swarming with U-boat wolf packs, which torpedoed merchant ships with little regard for their flags of registry, and in these encounters American seamen were blown up or drowned or died of exposure on unrescued life rafts.

Few Americans knew about these losses to their merchant shipping, because such figures were classified information. But the people of Mississippi's Gulf Coast knew something was happening. Freight rates for shipping had doubled and doubled again. A subsidized program of shipbuilding had been launched, and yards were swamped with orders for naval and merchant vessels, British and American. Roosevelt had set a goal for the construction of 8 million tons of shipping per year, an unheard-of total.

Then one Sunday morning in December 1941, war itself seized the United States. The only way America could participate was by way of her ships, carrying men, fuel, weapons, and supplies to the battlefields of a two-ocean war.

Jac Smith was in high school at the time of Pearl Harbor. He turned eighteen in 1942 and knew the draft would catch him soon. Like a lot of restless youngsters, he didn't want to wait until he was called up.

All around him, he saw and felt the excitement of a nation arming herself. Among the orders pouring in to Ingalls was one from Britain for four "baby" aircraft carriers, the H.M.SS. *BATTLER, HUNTER, CHASER,* and *PURSUER.* Fast, newly designed hulls, which had been intended for merchant ships, were fitted instead with flight decks and superstructures. As the carriers were readied, British crews were sent to Mississippi to man them and were housed in the only available quarters, abandoned CCC (Civil Conservation Corps) barracks in Magnolia Park near Ocean Springs. The Smiths, like many families on the Coast, invited the newcomers into their homes. Jac listened to their talk of convoy duty, the need for American supplies, and the fact that Britain could not hold out without help. He made up his mind.

Shortly after that visit, O. M. Smith, Jr. informed his family that he was going to join the Merchant Marine. He made the announcement calmly at the dinner table. After he had heard all the arguments about why he should reconsider, and after his mother's tears had dried, he said it again, quietly but firmly: "Mama, I'm going to sea."

Early the next morning he walked half a block to the railroad station and caught an L & N train to New Orleans. The cars were crowded with businessmen, soldiers, sailors, a family or two, and a group of Catholic nuns. Jack watched the morning light shimmering on the Gulf waters as the train clacked across the wooden trestle that spanned Bay Saint Louis, then trundled, steam whistle blowing, past Waveland, Clermont Harbor, English Lookout, the Pearl River, the narrow spit of land between Lake Pontchartrain and Lake Borgne. There were rows of fishing camps along both sides of the track, and the train stopped there to pick up passengers who flagged it down for a lift into town. Then at the foot of Canal Street, they reached the terminal: New Orleans.

Jac strolled down Canal marveling at the numbers of people of all kinds crowding the sidewalks, pouring in and out of the great stores, stepping on and off the street cars, crossing the intersections in never-ending streams—men in the uniforms of all the armed forces, ladies smart in hats and gloves. And private cars! Gasoline and tires were rationed, many automobiles had been put up on blocks for the duration, but one could not tell it by the traffic on Canal Street. It was all a little too grand for his taste, he decided.

He made his way to the stately Customs House at the corner of Canal and Decatur, and waited his turn to sign up in the U.S. Maritime Service. The historic New Orleans Customs House had high ceilings and wide halls in the tradition of Washington's federal architecture. Jac had felt small as he entered the building through the massive doors to the lobby. Climbing the stairs to the second floor, he heard the lonely echos of his own footsteps bouncing off the cold hard interior walls and ceiling. Arrows with the words "Merchant Marine" clearly marked the way to the room in which he now sat. Three or four men were ahead of him when he arrived, and several more came in while he waited. Some were about his age, some much older. As the line moved down the row of chairs, Jac reached the point of no return. If he filled out the application volunteering him for service in the Merchant Marine, he would soon be on his way to a training facility, leaving behind family, friends, home. If he turned around and walked out, nothing. He accepted the forms handed to him, walked to one of several tables in the room, and picked up one of the pencils lying there.

After completing all the forms, he had a couple of hours to spare before the next train home. He stood on the Customs House steps. It was spring, the azaleas in bud, and New Orleans at her best. Kept warm by the Mississippi on one side and Lake Pontchartrain on the other, the Crescent City had a semitropical climate and displayed lush greenery in all seasons, but spring gave her an extra charm. Still, Jac was not drawn to beautiful St. Charles Avenue, lined with graceful mansions and moss-decked oaks. Even the famous French Quarter did not lure him. Instead, he headed straight down Canal to the river and gazed at the vast numbers of merchant ships docked there, loading and unloading, at the endless stream of vessels steaming slowly downriver in midstream.

I'm going to be part of that, he thought.

In late afternoon, he caught the commuter train home. It was even more crowded than the morning train, but he managed to find a seat. He had not had time to eat lunch and was hungry, so he bought a stale sandwich from the vender and ate it slowly.

Across from him four servicemen, ties loosened, feet propped up, were sleeping off their New Orleans leave. He could smell the sour whisky. Up ahead a group of older business commuters were playing poker, telling jokes, and producing a cloud of cigar smoke. Jac opened his window. The odor of coal smoke streamed in with the cool air, and little drifts of soot accumulated on the window sill, but it was better than stale whisky and cigars.

The train chuffed to a halt at Bay St. Louis, Pass Christian, Longbeach, Gulfport, Edgewater, and finally Biloxi. Dozens of soldiers, duffel bags on their shoulders, poured off the train and into trucks waiting to take them to Keesler Army Air Field. Jac followed them off the train and walked home, feeling older and more worldly than he had that morning. He had a purpose now. He was going to sea.

Four Dollars, Thirty-Five Cents
and a Sack Lunch

The sea was hungry for men. Five days after he returned from New Orleans, Jac received a letter telling him to report to a new maritime training facility recently established at St. Petersburg, Florida. The U.S. Maritime Service was a branch of the War Shipping Administration. Its mission was to instruct large numbers of men in seamanship and prepare them for life at sea—as quickly as possible. The trainees would wear uniforms and serve under a military discipline, but once graduated they would be civilian merchant seamen, working for the companies whose ships had been requisitioned for war service. It was a dangerous life, whose contribution to the war effort would never be fully understood by the public.

Jac packed a few clothes and went to the kitchen to say good-bye. He could never remember his mother not being in the kitchen. Today she was all pride and briskness, keeping back the tears. "Here, you'll need this—it's all we have in the house." She gave him four dollars and thirty-five cents, and added a sandwich in a brown paper bag.

His father tried to say something, couldn't, and shook his son's hand instead. It would be a long time before the Smiths saw their son again.

It may be hard for people today to realize how unprepared for war the United States was in 1942. Her armed forces, although enlarged by the peacetime draft, were still relatively small in number and poorly equipped. Her torpedoes didn't work, her carrier aircraft were outclassed by the Zeros, she had lost half her surface navy at Pearl Harbor. But she was the only major nation in the world whose industry was not under armed attack, and it was on the boil. Shipyards for the first time were applying the principles of mass production to shipbuilding. In 1939–1940 only 102 ships of all types were built in the United States; by the end of 1942, 646 merchant vessels had come off the ways. The work force lost many of its young men to the Army and Navy, so older workers were brought out of retirement, and women entered the shipyards. At Ingalls, welding torches sparked, cranes swung sheets of iron, and the gates boasted laconic signs: "Launching today."

But who was to sail these countless new vessels? How could a merchant marine of barely 50,000 experienced seamen be quickly expanded to one of 200,000?

First every old salt who would volunteer, regardless of age, was recruited to help. They packed their old seabags once more and forgot their stiff joints and tired sea legs. Many were glad for the chance to walk the decks again and show the young whippersnappers what being a seaman meant. Second, the age limit for merchant seamen was lowered to sixteen, so that the shippers could recruit from a younger age group than the armed forces. Third, recruiting posters were distributed far and wide, playing the age-old siren song of the sea.

In six short weeks, these youthful volunteers were taught the basics of seamanship. Then they were sent to sea, where the *real* training took place. They learned from experienced seamen—some only a year or two older than themselves, some belonging to their grandfathers' generation. By the time they reached that first destination—if they reached it—they were experienced seamen themselves, and, probably, combat veterans.

During his basic training Jac drew the attention of the training staff at St. Petersburg under the command of Captain Hollie J. Tiedemann. The boy could listen, learn, and take orders. He could, it was observed, also teach and give orders. He was promoted to coxswain and made an instructor of lifeboat training and abandon-ship drills aboard the old three-masted sailing ship *Joseph Conrad* (now on permanent display at Mystic Harbor, Connecticut).

Jac was young but not inexperienced with boats. He had done his share of offshore fishing and oystering. It was not hard for a young man who grew up in hurricane country to imagine the difficulty of launching and manning lifeboats from a sinking ship in a rough sea. He took his training duties seriously. Soon, he gained a reputation for being a hard taskmaster. He believed that these new recruits had to be toughened and limbered up, if they were to survive the hazards of convoy duty that lay ahead.

Jac's daily classes began with mast climbing. He made recruits climb the rat lines from the deck to the trucks of the masthead, up the starboard side, down the port side—all three masts, one after the other without stopping—and then back into formation. Next came the vital lessons in abandoning ship, lifeboat handling, rowing, wire and rope splicing, and general seamanship. Jac taught his charges the basics of lifeboat construction, emergency gear, sailing, and rowing. Launching a boat is a demanding and exacting job. If it is poorly done under demanding sea conditions, a boat and crew can be smashed to bits. Regardless of sea conditions, regardless of whether the ship is burning, sinking, or under fire, the boats must be quickly and safely launched if they were to be launched at all. And launching didn't end the emergency. There was the matter of grabbing an oar and rowing. Coordination comes hard for a green crew, and rowing in cadence is not easily learned. It takes patience on the instructor's part and practice on the crew's. And yet this is a vital skill, too. When the crew abandons ship—especially a burning tanker or ammunition ship—they must pull away swiftly if they are not to be sucked down into the vortex of the sinking vessel.

Once rowing was learned, it was time to break out and rig the boat's sail. Teaching men to sail took even more patience than teaching them to row. In the beginning it was more like a clowns' circus fire drill, but after several members of a new crew had their heads cracked by the boom or were swept over the side when the boat gybed unexpectedly, they soon settled down and learned how to use the force of wind on a sail. The sail had two other uses. One came in handy when they were becalmed in the middle of Tampa Bay under a blazing noon sun. They learned to use the sail as a shelter. Jac also taught them how to rig it so it caught and collected rainwater, which could mean life or death to a shipwrecked crew without water rations.

Jac's classes graduated with calluses on their hands, muscles in their arms, legs, and backs, and brains stuffed with useful and necessary knowledge. They rowed across Tampa Bay in all kinds of weather. They handled the deck tackle for launching the boats. They could launch boats, row them, rig and sail them, and use and maintain all safety and emergency gear aboard ship. They could find every piece of gear and rations aboard the boat blindfolded, from blankets to bailer, sea anchor to storm oil, water and food to first aid pack. Such training is not an outing in a rowboat.

At St. Petersburg the commander decided it was time to see how much had been learned. He announced that a grand lifeboat race would be held—for volunteers. Each instructor could hand-pick the crew that would represent him from those who had entered. On the day that the crews were to be chosen, all the divisions were marched to the boat dock and lined up. Instructors looked over their choices. Every man who had trained under Jac had volunteered. As he walked down the lines of men and pointed out ten of them, he could see grins on the faces of the chosen.

The event was well publicized, and on the chosen day thousands of friends, sweethearts, and families lined the St. Petersburg yacht basin. The boats were launched, and their crews pulled away for the starting line. Jac restrained his crew, telling them to row easy; no need to expend energy before they got to the starting line. Fifteen boats drew up in a line across the basin.

Jac, sitting at the tiller, cupped hands around his mouth. "When you hear the gun, give it all you've got. You men are the best there is."

At the starting gun, Coxswain Smith's boat pulled out to a three-boat-lengths lead and kept it all the way to the finish line. "When I gave the command, 'Rest oars,' we were the proudest bunch of men in town," Jac recalled long afterward. As his personal reward, he was tossed into Tampa Bay by his victorious crew.*

These merchant seamen needed all the fun they could get ashore, because little was waiting for them at sea. Losses had climbed to as high as 500,000 tons of shipping in one month. The hard training they had received from Jac Smith and other dedicated instructors might come in desperately handy all too soon.

Because he was a skilled instructor, Jac was given students of a different sort: Russian sailors, who had been sent to St. Petersburg for training. Smith was assigned to teach them deck and lifeboat drills, and gunnery. American merchant ships were now armed for antisub and antiaircraft defense—20 mm machine guns plus 5-inch 38s (5 inches in bore, 38 calibers in length) and 3-inch 50s.

The Russians were billeted in the confiscated Sarena Hotel, only a short walk from the training station. They arrived in the Florida heat wearing heavy wool winter uniforms, and although they were rough, young, husky, and well disciplined, the heat and humidity nearly killed them. They were held as virtual prisoners by their Russian commander, carefully iso-

---

* The official Maritime Service newspaper said, "Representing Division 195, these eleven stalwarts brought their boat across the finish line ahead of 14 other boats in the lifeboat race for Maritime trainees at the Vinoy hotel in Vinoy basin. Members of the crew are: O. M. Smith, coxswain, Biloxi, Miss.; W. C. (Buddy) Bell, Statesville, N.C.; Madison F. Lee, Lakeland, Fla.; Charles B. Peterson, Tampa; Norman L. Wicks, Norfolk, Va.; Bill Bauton, Lakeland; V. J. Early, New Martinsville, West Va.; Joe W. Walters, Charleston, S.C.; Wilbur N. Willis, Tifton, Ga.; and Pete Remine, Knoxville, Tenn. Prizes were awarded to the first three boats."

lated from the American seamen. Daily, they were marched to the *Joseph Conrad,* where they were turned over to Jac. He taught them, mostly with sign language that he made up as he went along, since their interpreter could not speak very much English. At the end of the day, they were marched directly back to the Sarena. They were not allowed out, and no one was allowed in, and the hotel was guarded by Russian foot patrols armed with machine guns. Their political officer was always on hand to prevent any exchange of friendship. Finally, their training completed, they were shipped out.

Harm's Way

Smith soon tired of instructor duty. He requested and was granted sea duty.

Jac had no exact knowledge at the time of just what lay ahead. He knew the duty was hazardous, but he thought in romantic terms—the glamorous, heroic danger of boyhood stories.

The truth was known only to those already at sea. The North Atlantic itself was often more deadly than the enemy torpedoes and bombs. If the order was given to abandon ship, the crew had only minutes to reach the relative safety of a lifeboat or raft before the cold incapacitated their muscles and they died from hypothermia or drowned. Those in lifeboats faced days or weeks—or longer—of isolation on cold and stormy seas. There were many occasions when crews escaped injury but could not survive the sea in their lifeboats. The S.S. *Cado,* a Socony-Vacuum tanker, was torpedoed in November of 1942. All of the forty-two crewmen and seventeen naval armed guards survived the sinking and successfully launched and boarded three lifeboats. Of those fifty-nine souls, only six survived the freezing and stormy sea.

When a ship was hit, all the crew was exposed to terrible injury, but especially those manning the ship's engines down below, the black gang.* When engine rooms took a direct hit, they turned into horror chambers of broken steam lines, exploding boilers, and flaming fuel, scalding and burning the trapped stokers far below decks.

Every American truck, tank, ship, and plane—and most of those of our allies, including the Soviet Union—ran on fuel transported to the war zones by tankers. Tankermen knew their chances in the cold water, but their greatest fear was of fire. The tankers were loaded low in the water with cargoes of high test gasoline or oil. When hit, a tanker usually became an inferno, isolating crewmen from escape or preventing the launching of lifeboats. Even when lifeboats or rafts were launched successfully, the sea around them could erupt in flames as millions of gallons of petroleum poured onto the water and ignited. Men leaped from flaming decks into seas on fire. There were occasions when lifeboats and their passengers, well clear of their burning ship, were still set on fire when oil blown high into the air by explosions on board the stricken vessel ignited and fell from the sky like burning rain.

The men who sailed the merchant ships were civilians, seamen making a living for themselves and their families, volunteers. They had no military obligations. No one could order

* In sea jargon "black" has nothing to do with race but refers to the sooty faces of stokers who in early days shoveled coal all day long into the fireboxes of ships. Diesel engines have replaced coal, but men working in the engine rooms are still called the black gang.

them into harm's way. But they went just the same. Transporting cargo was their job. Those who survived one convoy sailed on the next one—and the one after that. Some were terribly wounded, some died by fire, some by ice. Over six hundred were taken prisoner by the Germans and Japanese. At least three were placed in a prison camp near the Arctic Circle by the bureaucracy of an ungrateful Stalinist Russia. One of them was a Mississippian.

Seamen were hired out to man merchant vessels through their union and seaman halls. A company needing a crew for a certain vessel, requisitioned for government service, called the halls and requested the number of men of such-and-such qualifications required. Those men registered for jobs the longest went first, always on a "destination unknown" basis.

Jac was told that Philadelphia was a good place to be hired on quickly. Crews were desperately needed for the T-2 tankers being turned out by the Sun Shipyard.

It was a long train trip from St. Petersburg to Philadelphia, and was as far as Jac had ever traveled from home. When he got there, he found Philadelphia awash in Navy sailors and merchant seamen. The Naval Yard and all docks and shipyards in the area were crowded with ships of every description and in every stage of building, repair, outfitting, and loading. The arcs of welding torches flared brightly day and night. Trucks lined the streets waiting to load or unload at the docks. Cranes hefted cargo of every description aboard ship. There was one message in the air: *Hurry.* Europe has fallen, England is in peril, Hitler is at the gates of Moscow—*Hurry.*

Jac checked in at the Seaman's Hall to await ship assignment, then hastened out to buy his outfit. Merchant seamen furnished their own clothing, and he had a long list: wool shirts, wool pants, long underwear (no insulated longjohns in those days), warm leather boots, rubber sea boots, foul weather gear, a heavy sheepskin coat, gloves, and mittens. That list completed, he loaded up on what medical supplies he thought he might need.

The only ones available aboard most merchant ships at the time were iodine, castor oil, and cotton. Whatever ailed you, you used iodine or castor oil—it was a real incentive not to get sick. The captain or the officer in charge of the naval armed guard usually had a sea chest equipped with morphine, splints, sutures, and other supplies for serious wounds or injuries, but with ordinary ills you were pretty much on your own. A merchant ship's "designated hospital" might be a paint locker or other storage area used mostly for on-going poker games. When a ship had a real sick bay, it was often requisitioned as quarters for the naval armed guard, or a place to store clean linen until it was needed.

Three days after arriving in Philadelphia Jac had a ship assignment. No time to visit Independence Hall or gaze at the Liberty Bell. He packed his gear and a few personal belongings in a sea bag he had sewn himself out of heavy canvas, and took a bus to the Sun Shipyard in nearby Chester. There he boarded a new T-2 tanker, the *Cedar Creek*. He opened up a book, looked up her specifications, and began to learn his ship.

T-2 TANKER SPECIFICATIONS

Length 523′ 6″
Beam 68′
Draft 30′
Net Tonnage 6,107
Dead Weight Tonnage 16,765

Propulsion, Turbo-Electric, 6,000 hp.
Speed 16 knots
Cruising Range 12,500 miles
Liquid Cargo Capacity 90,000 barrels
Armament: (1) 3″ fifty gun on the bow.
          (1) 5″ thirty eight on the stern.
          (4) 20 mm. machine guns on the bridge.
          (4) 20 mm. machine guns on the stern.
Crew: Merchant Marine—42 officers & men
      Armed Naval Guard—17, including one officer, usually a
      lieutenant jg.

Jac didn't know much about the naval armed guard, but he would learn a lot in the years to come. Up to sixteen sailors and one officer were assigned to each merchant ship to man the 3- and 4-inch guns mounted fore and aft in gun tubs, and various machine guns, usually mounted on the bridge and stern.

On shore there was occasional friction between Navy men and merchant seamen, generally because of pay differences. The sailors received a maximum of only $64 to $78 a month, some much less. The merchant seamen, paid by the ship's owner for whom they worked, received more than twice that amount, plus bonus pay for war duty, the amount depending on which area they sailed to.

However, aboard ship, the average merchant seaman and the average Navy man got along like old neighborhood friends—shipmates. They shared the same fear, same battles, same determination to take the ship through. Merchant deck crews passed ammunition to naval gunners, and took their places if they fell, as many did.

The guns often proved vital to a ship's survival, keeping enemy planes at a respectable distance, fighting off submarines during surface attacks. Running gun battles were fierce.

Naval gunners often refused to abandon a sinking ship as long as they could fire their weapons. They suffered the same fate as the merchant seamen, and in the North Atlantic, their units suffered higher casualties than any in the Navy.

Smith joined the newly formed crew of the *Cedar Creek.* Normally he would have come aboard expecting no more than to earn his AB (Able Bodied Seaman) papers. But times were not normal. His record as an instructor aboard the *Joseph Conrad* was enough to win him a slot as acting boatswain, responsible for the deck crew of twelve men. They handled and maintained all deck machinery, winches, anchor windlasses, lifeboats and tackle, mast and boom machinery. At battle stations, some were assigned to stand by to launch lifeboats, others to aid the armed guard by passing ammunition up to the guns. Jac was familiar with it all and knew his job. The voyage would determine if he'd retain the rating permanently.

The *Cedar Creek* was owned by the Marine Transport Line, and her captain's name was Gustav Svenson. Captain Svenson, now age seventy, had been born in Sweden. Many of the older seamen were Scandinavian, carrying on a mastery of the North Atlantic that dated back to the Vikings, and any seaman was lucky to serve with them. Jac knew that if he was a good enough boatswain for Captain Svenson, he was a good enough boatswain for anyone.

Once crew and ship were united, no time was wasted. The *Cedar Creek* had already been assigned to a convoy assembling in New York. The new ship was taken on a six-hour trial run down the frost-rimmed Delaware at night. It was late December, 1943. The deck crew was required to stand by the anchor windlass at all times during the trial run, ready to let go the anchors should the new ship lose power or steering. The crew stood regular four-hour watches, but the young boatswain was required to stand by the entire time. Smith remembers how cold he was that night. There would be many times in the future when he would be colder, but that was the first time the boy from Biloxi had ever been in freezing weather aboard ship.

The words of a saying of the day occurred to the half-frozen young boatswain: "All Southern boys are sent to the North Atlantic to shiver and shake, and all the Northern boys are sent to the South Pacific to burn and bake." The deck machinery was operated by steam so that the deck crews standing by could at least warm their hands on the steam lines that fed them. But up ahead the forward lookouts and the gunners shivered in the frozen night—they had no steam lines on which to warm their hands. Jac wondered just what he had gotten himself into.

But he was not so cold that he could not pause to recognize the vast beauty of winter on the Delaware. A good part of the estuary was frozen over, and the moon nearly at the full. White snow and ice sharply contrasted with dark water, inlets defined in the distance by sharp white lines against black. And there were more ducks than he had ever seen, ducks clearly visible in the soft lunar light. He wondered if they planned to spend the winter in this frozen landscape. He wondered how much colder his own winter would get.

The *Cedar Creek* floated, the screw turned, and the cook could cook. The inspectors pronounced the ship fit and ready for sea. She was loaded with liquid cargo, and ordered to New York. Not until she was en route up the East Coast was a problem discovered.

Ships were equipped with what was called a degaussing system, which consisted of electrical cables fixed to the outside of the hull, through which an electric current was passed. The system was supposed to counteract the magnetic field of the steel ship to prevent it from setting off magnetic mines and torpedoes. The seamen didn't believe it worked. Moreover, in the case of the *Cedar Creek,* workmen at the shipyard had failed to pack and seal the holes in the side of the hull where the cable entered the ship, which in this case was into the crew's quarters. As a result, icy Atlantic water constantly leaked through the holes, covering the deck of the crew's quarters inches deep.

Jumping out of bunks into three or four inches of ice water was a sure-fire cure for drowsiness. Clothing, lifejackets, and bed coverings were one big cold soggy mess all the way to New York.

After a brief stop at Todd Shipyard in Brooklyn to correct the cabin leak, the *Cedar Creek,* loaded with high-test gasoline, proceeded up the river and anchored just off Grant's Tomb at about 125th Street, to await assembly of her convoy. Jac, with a few hours to spend ashore, did what any schoolboy might do on his first trip to New York. He went to see that "damn Yankee general's tomb." He caught the afternoon liberty boat back to the ship and later that night watched from the after deck as the *Cedar Creek* left the skyline of the great city behind and proceeded through the submarine nets protecting the vast and vital harbors of New York–New Jersey. Outside the sea buoy, they joined a small coastal convoy, headed up the sea lanes to Halifax, Nova Scotia, and anchored to await the formation of the large convoy to Britain.

Convoy

Early in the war, Britain had instituted the practice, invented in World War I, of moving merchant ships by convoy, escorted by as many naval vessels as could be spared. This did not guarantee safety for the cargo carriers, but it cut down on losses.

When the United States first entered the war, coastal shipping was still carried by single ships, traveling to Halifax or St. John's on their own. Then a hard lesson was learned. In early 1942, Admiral Karl Doenitz, commander of Germany's submarine fleet, dispatched a small pack of U-boats, perhaps a dozen or so, to patrol the American coast from the Canadian border to Texas. Of the 441 Allied merchant ships lost between January and May of that year, eighty-seven were sunk in American waters, most within sight of shore.

Many of these victim ships had been clearly silhouetted against the bright lights of the cities along the coast—cities which at first refused to adopt blackout procedures, because that would hurt their resort business. The orange glow from flaming ships, plus the oil and charred bodies that began to wash ashore on their beaches, changed their attitudes. Now, with coastal cities blacked out and ships moving cautiously in small convoys, merchant vessels converged in greater safety on the two principal Canadian ports.

Halifax, with her ten-square-mile anchorage, was well suited to the formation of convoys. Her docks were jammed with every kind of supplies imaginable, matériel brought in by truck, rail, barge, and coastal freighters for transfer to those ships not already loaded to their limits. Her shipyards were full of vessels undergoing repair. Crowding her pubs was the most diverse crowd of seamen in the world: Canadians, Englishmen, Scots, Americans, Norwegians, Free Poles, Dutchmen, Swedes, Danes, a Free Frenchman or two, and a small batch of East Indians, Arabs, and Chinese. Every pub was a boozing Tower of Babel.

Halifax knew her job, for she had served the same function during World War I. But she performed it with caution and a well-founded underlying anxiety. In December 1917 a ship laden with ammunition had blown sky high, killing thousands of people. Whether the result of accident or sabotage, such a disaster was a very real hazard to every port of embarkation during wartime.

Seamen granted brief shore leave before shipping out didn't waste time worrying about danger here in port. Halifax offered them lobster, beer, whisky, tall tales, laughter, and sweet-smelling ladies of the night, and they plunged in to enjoy it all. Jac Smith was not far behind his shipmates. Young, wide-eyed, his innocence showing, he followed where the more experienced led. There would be plenty to worry about once the convoy was formed and they headed out into the black Atlantic.

U-boats were waiting out there for the slow-moving convoys.

T-2 tankers and some of the modern merchant ships could make sixteen knots or better, often fast enough to evade or outdistance a submarine. But a convoy had to proceed at the speed of the slowest vessel. Ships were so desperately needed that anything that could float was put into service, and some of them could barely make nine knots. Even with a clean bottom, a new Liberty ship would do well to make eleven knots in a calm sea.

By 1943 Germany had between 500 and 700 submarines. They were 375 feet long, carried twenty torpedoes, a 4-inch deck gun, and deck machine guns. They had a range of 15,000 miles. Underwater, powered by batteries, a U-boat could travel only eight knots, but a sleek sub running on the surface with diesel engines could easily make sixteen knots or more. Moreover, a sub on the surface could not be detected by the sonar sets of the day; reliable surface radar had not been perfected. It is easy to see why their favorite tactic, against a convoy forced to plod along at nine knots, was a night attack on the surface.

Sailing orders had come. Like most, Jac had a bit of trouble lifting his poor aching head and carrying it on deck the morning after his good time. An icy blast of Canadian air helped clear his head as he assembled a badly hungover work party. They checked all deck gear and machinery, lashings, hatches, and tank-access covers, stowed away all loose items and tools in their respective places. By noon all preparations for getting under way were complete. Down below the black gang, under the watchful eye of the chief engineer, was raising a full head of steam. There was nothing to do now but wait.

As darkness slid over the harbor, Jac moved a work party forward to the bow. They were about to weigh anchor. Steadily the clanking windlass drew the great muddy chain out of the hawse pipe, and the anchor rose from the harbor floor, links sparking fire as they contacted the chain-hoist drum. To the bridge he signaled, "Anchors aweigh."

The harbor pilot, standing with the captain on the port wing of the bridge, called, "Ten degrees port rudder, all ahead slow," and *Cedar Creek* joined the line of ships moving out to the Atlantic. At the sea buoy the harbor pilot climbed down a rope ladder and onto the waiting pilot boat that would transport him back to Halifax. Several of the crew standing at the forecastle head, Jac among them, watched him depart. As he reached the deck below, he shouted up to those on the bridge, "God speed you, gentleman." An old salt standing next to Jac whispered, "Amen."

The pilot boat, showing no lights, turned for home and disappeared against the dark horizonless curtain. The East Coast of Canada was entirely blacked out, not a light to be seen under an overcast starless night. No silhouetting these ships. That was the moment when Jac, standing alone in the cold of early January 1943, knew the preliminaries were over. They were bound across a cold and hostile sea.

Convoy duty in the North Atlantic was a serious business, governed by tough and unforgiving rules. They began ashore. Merchant seamen soon learned that "loose lips" did indeed "sink ships." The Germans were suspected of receiving very accurate information on the departure dates and times for outbound convoys. Survivors of sunken subs reported that they often not only knew a convoy's departure time, but the names of the ships assigned to it and the cargo they carried. One bold U-boat skipper, after sinking a merchant ship at night off the New Jersey coast, came alongside a lifeboat of survivors and chided them in English: "You were two hours late. We had a long wait for you." Then he saluted and returned to his undersea world.

Sabotage was another deadly threat. On one convoy within a period of twenty minutes, the steering cables on two different ships parted, causing loss of control. The result was one collision and another near miss. Crewmen aboard both crippled vessels reported that the steering cables had been sawed three quarters of the way through. Some ships had to drop out of convoy because of fuel lines fouled by foreign material deliberately dumped into fuel tanks. It could take hours to clear the problem and relight the boilers. Any ship that had to drop out of the convoy ran a very high risk. The subs, which almost always followed the convoys at a safe distance, were waiting for just such an opportunity.

For their own safety, and that of their convoys, the merchant seamen were not told in advance when or where they would sail. They would report to their union halls or the Maritime Administration offices and get an assignment to a ship. There was never much of a waiting period.

Only ship captains, executive officers, naval armed guard officers, and captains of naval and Coast Guard escort vessels were cleared to attend convoy briefings. These were conducted by the convoy commodore, an experienced merchant captain, often British, and at them information was distributed as to destination, route, departure date and time, ship convoy station assignments, zigzag signals, weather, and other data necessary for safe passage. Code signal books were passed around with a sincere "God speed."

Convoys usually left port under cover of darkness, slipping ship by ship through the submarine nets laid across the entrance to ports. The nets were opened by special harbor vessels to let friendly shipping in or out.

Outbound ships would form into convoy in a predetermined area, usually outside the sea buoy. Ships were assigned stations in columns spaced 3,000 feet apart, one ship behind the other at 1,500 foot intervals. Because the greatest exposure was from the side, columns were usually limited to five ships. Thus a thirty-ship convoy would be composed of six columns, five ships to a column, a fifty ship convoy to ten columns of five ships each. A ship assigned the station of 5–4 would be in column five, the fourth ship in line. Tankers and ammunition ships were usually given the most protection and placed inside the convoy, spaced carefully so that they were never adjacent to one another. If they were spaced too closely, a hit on one might create a chain reaction—one exploding ship setting off another.

Though simple in theory, a convoy is anything but simple in practice. It is very difficult to maintain a ship's assigned station, even in calm seas. Slow sailors tended to lag behind, fast vessels to go too fast. Add to this stormy seas or nightly blackouts or heavy fog or blowing snow. Or the icebergs or attack by submarines or aircraft. Moreover, merchant ships did not have the benefit of surface radar, which did not appear even in the naval escort vessels until well into 1943. As late as two weeks before Germany's surrender, submarines were still sinking ships off America's coast.

To make things more difficult for the subs, a convoy constantly zigzagged. At random intervals, the convoy commodore would signal maneuver commands by flag hoist or blinker—white by day, red by night. Maneuver command included the type of turn and heading, then the signal "execute." And the convoy changed course. Any ship failing to follow directions would pose a very real danger of collision.

Radio silence was mandatory. The enemy was well skilled in radio direction-finding procedures. A radio transmission from a ship would immediately give him the convoy's position. Receiving messages was all right—usually from admiralty headquarters on shore: new orders, weather, enemy positions. But these could not be acknowledged. Even if a ship in distress radioed for help, no ship in the convoy would answer. Instead distress signals were acted upon by rescue vessels assigned to a convoy.

It is an extremely demanding task to maintain a station 1,500 feet behind the ship in front of you, and 3,000 feet from ships on either side of you on a dark night with all ships blacked out. Now add fog so thick you cannot see the bow of your own ship from the bridge. True, you have the last heading you were given, and you haven't changed your speed, but how about the ship in front, or behind, or on either side? You are loaded with aviation gasoline. If you show a light, you will endanger the entire convoy to enemy attack.

One aid to help ships stay in line without running down the ship in front of them was a simple device called a fog buoy. This was usually made out of a spar or length of pipe with an up-turned spout fashioned in such a way that when towed on the end of a thousand feet of cable it would throw up a spray of water visible to the bow lookout on the vessel following behind. As long as the lookout could see the spray from the fog buoy, his ship could remain in line at a safe distance. It might be as lost as the ship in front, but it wouldn't run over it.

Jac was responsible for fog buoys aboard his ship and was often awakened at all hours to set or retrieve one as the need might be. He used anything handy to make fog buoys: four-by-four timbers, pipe stock, even an empty oil drum, towed end on. Attached to its cable and released, this crude device became an effective warning marker.

The story is told of a relatively new captain and crew the first time they saw a fog buoy used. Suddenly they went to full speed and pulled up alongside the ship in front, scaring its captain half to death. The green captain, using his megaphone, shouted out for him to open fire with his stern cannon on the submarine following just behind. After the captain of the front ship explained that the "sub" was a fog buoy, rigged to make it easier for the second vessel to follow, the much embarrassed captain thanked him and sheepishly returned his ship to station.

In spite of all the procedures, convoys were occasionally scattered. Days of Arctic fog could do it, or a field of icebergs, enemy attack, or waves forty feet high driven by snow-laden gale-force winds. Collisions did happen, and ships separated from the protection of the convoy often disappeared forever. Convoy duty anywhere was rarely fun. Convoy duty in the North Atlantic was one of the most hazardous wartime duties anywhere.

The *Cedar Creek* was assigned the 2–2 position, second ship in the second column. Her mostly new crew was too busy settling down to shipboard routine to worry much about the crossing.

For those who sail for a living the ship becomes home. They work on her, sleep on her, do their laundry, have their meals, spend their free time. They form friendships, sometimes enmities. Every man learns that everyone aboard depends upon him to do his job. Whether likeable or not, those who do their jobs well are respected by the rest of the crew. Those who don't become outcasts. A ship and its crew can be endangered or lost by what a single crewman does or fails to do. Steal something from a shipmate, he might try to kill you, but if you need something he has, he'll probably give it to you. Most seamen never forget the other men with whom they have sailed.

The Cold

From Halifax they made their way toward Iceland. The few escorts they had, some Navy, some Coast Guard, were seen one day to turn back toward North America flying a flag signal that said, "Good-bye and good luck." The crew was at first alarmed, but soon realized that the convoy was simply being handed over to a new Navy escort sent out from Iceland. This was why convoys were routed so far north. It forced them to sail into the freezing stormy seas of the Arctic Circle, but it also brought them within protective range of land-based aircraft.

In the 1930's the German Karl Haushofer wrote, "Whoever possesses Iceland holds a pistol pointed at England, America, and Canada." Denmark, a neutral country when war broke out, ruled Iceland. When Germany invaded Denmark in 1940, England quickly seized control of the island, which lay within easy reach of her lifeline shipping routes. (Had Germany done so instead, the effort to keep Great Britain supplied might have failed.) Five months before America officially entered the war, she sent armed forces into Iceland to relieve the 24,000 British troops stationed there, which were desperately needed in North Africa. Iceland provided a base where escort vessels could refuel and from which rescue vessels could sweep the fields of wreckage behind the convoys in search of survivors. Most important of all, it supplied airfields for long-range patrol planes.

Jac Smith began to learn the meaning of cold. Repeatedly his deck crew had to chip away tons of ice that formed on the railings, equipment, and rigging. They made, tended, launched, and retrieved fog buoys. Under submarine warnings, or actual attack, they had to stand by the lifeboats, ready to launch them.

The water temperature could hover at, or even below, freezing. Ocean spray turned instantly to ice when it came in contact with anything on the exposed topsides. Such ice was called black frost by the fishermen of the North Sea. When their crews could not hack it away fast enough, boats have capsized under the weight. Rigging, machinery, rails, decks, guns, masts, and deck cargo became encrusted with ice. So did the lookouts, deck gang, and gunners. Norsemen had a saying about the North Atlantic and North Sea: "They are too salty to freeze and too cold not to."

Smith wore four or five pairs of pants, equal layers of shirts and sweaters, his heavy sheepskin coat, sea boots, gloves, and a newly issued zoot suit. Still, he nearly froze to death.

By 1943 crews were issued slick innertubelike rubber suits. They were quickly dubbed "zoot suits" after a clothing fad of the times. The rubber suits were made in one piece, head to toe, including a tight fitting hood, and were designed to be worn over all the clothing one could put on, plus a life jacket. The only way to get into them was through the collar which had a draw string that was pulled tight once you got inside. The feet of the suit were weighted with lead to prevent the suit's buoyancy from turning the wearer upside down in the water. It had pockets so a crewman could carry whatever personal survival items he deemed wise. It also had a whistle, knife, and small battery-powered red flashing light near the neck piece.

When some of the crew asked Jac to explain their use, he replied, "You use the light to be seen in dark waters, use the whistle to attract the attention of anyone who doesn't see the light, and use the knife to cut your throat if the first two don't work."

Zoot suits were uncomfortable and hard to move around in, and when exposed to freezing spray, they would ice up and become as stiff and heavy as a suit of armor. But if a man had to jump into the water, the zoot suit provided him with a few added minutes of life, maybe enough to reach a raft. Usually, captains gave standing orders requiring that the rubber suits be worn when under attack warnings. The men slept in them, ate in them, worked in them, hated them. But they wore them.

Submariners liked rough seas. They helped to hide the wake of the periscopes or even the conning towers if they were running on the surface. However, if seas were mountainous, that was an advantage to the convoys, for the U-boatmen were prevented from seeing their targets, even when a convoy was near. For this reason, merchant crews maintained a love-hate relationship with Atlantic storms.

As the *Cedar Creek*'s convoy drove eastward, the North Atlantic was ruled by angry weather. One deep depression after another swept down upon them, pounding the convoy with merciless gales. All efforts of crews were directed at surviving the elements. Fighting off U-boats became secondary.

Such weather chose no sides. The captains and crews of the U-boats endured the same nightmare conditions as Jac's men. To have any hope of sighting the enemy, they could not stay below the surface in the relative calm. They had to run on the surface through the raging seas. Their conning towers were engulfed by breakers, the crew on watch barely having time to recover from one wet bashing before the next was on them. A submarine's log book often recorded without exaggeration, "Crew coming off watch half frozen and nearly drowned."

Stowaway

There were times when the stress of the voyage was eased by camaraderie among crew members who, when off duty, gathered in the galley for meals, or maybe just for hot coffee and the company to be found there. The coffee came in special cans which had a victory ship, a tanker, and a liberty ship painted around them with the words "Coffee for Men of Action." The men thought the name was silly, but they liked the coffee. The way it was brewed on most ships, it could knock a mule to its knees.

In the galley some crewmembers talked to whoever was present. Others listened but rarely spoke. The mess served as community center, U.S.O., casino, and stage for the best liars on the ocean. There was enough bragging of outrageous sexcapades to fill an encyclopedia. Women and war usually vied for first place as favorite topics, but there was also simple talk of home and family, jokes and jibes and gripes and tall tales, arguments, sometimes a fight, and once in a while, a guarded confession of fear, or a knowing word of cheer when it was needed.

Sometimes something ridiculous would happen, a close call or foolish near accident. Telling about it could break the tension on the entire ship and keep the galley alive with laughter for days, lifting morale. The *Cedar Creek*'s stowaway provided many a tension breaker.

The stowaway was a poorly kept secret at first. One of the navy gunners, having had a few drinks in New York, bought a small, deceitful, vengeful, foul and obscene demon disguised as a monkey, and sneaked the thing aboard just before sailing. Like all clever demons, this one at first made himself the darling of the crew, happily snuggling in the arms of one and then another seaman, snatching a piece of personal gear here and there, wearing a sailor hat, eagerly accepting an offered bit of food, only occasionally biting the hell out of someone for the fun of it.

Of course, his presence was not known to all on board— the captain and other officers, for example, who rarely ventured to the crew's quarters astern. Therefore, the furry little alien was given residence in the gunners' tool room aft. He was put on a long chain and the porthole in the tool room, leading to the after gun deck, was left open. This afforded him a limited ability to promenade about the after gun deck. He became a great morale booster, except to the gunner who had brought him aboard. The gunner was unanimously elected to clean up the little deposits the creature left over the length and breadth of his domain. Often he would climb out of his porthole to the end of his chain and keep the gun crew company when they were at their station, braving the cold to do so. The creature was always present when parts were brought to the tool room for repair. There he would watch as tools were selected and applied to their respective use.

It was about mid-Atlantic when the gunners began to come to Jac to borrow tools. At first he thought nothing of it. Then when a tool or two was not returned, he got a little put out.

"I thought you fellows had your own special set of tools for the guns. Better tools than mine, as I remember."

"That's right, Boatswain, but I guess some of the fellows have misplaced a wrench or two."

"The hell they have! What do they think, that they can walk down to the hardware store and buy a replacement?"

"Beats me. But I got to tell you, I can't find that wrench I borrowed from you yesterday."

"Well, by damn, somebody better answer up for it or I'm gonna' use a hammer to jog some memories."

No one came up with the missing tools or even a clue to their disappearance. Then it dawned on Jac that the tools were disappearing from the monkey's sleeping quarters. A day or so later he got to the aft deck just in time to see the monkey give a gleeful heave to a pipe wrench, watching the splash as it disappeared into the deep six. Tool boxes and cabinets were thereafter locked.

However, the demon monkey was foiled for only a short while before his genius resulted in one of the strangest exchanges of signals ever made between a convoy commodore and one of the ships of his command.

The monkey saved his most outrageous trick for a particularly tense night. It was a rare occasion on the North Atlantic when the seas were relatively calm. This was a decided advantage for the U-boats cruising swiftly on the surface. In calm waters, they could more easily see and close on a convoy. It was a pitch black night, the kind where even a glowing cigarette could be seen for a mile. Every ship was totally blacked out. Every cabin had a blackout curtain besides a door guarding its entrance. Every cabin porthole was painted black. A light from a convoy could spell death by alerting a U-boat of its presence.

On this particular evening there had been a submarine warning just after sundown. Everyone was tense, especially the deck watch and gun crews on duty. Suddenly in the pitch-black night, a clear bright light blazed out from the *Cedar Creek!* It came from the porthole of the gunners' tool room.

The gunners fell all over themselves racing to the tool room to extinguish that stark white beacon before it could alert every enemy submarine in the Atlantic.

They were fast, but not fast enough. The convoy commodore was advised by signal from an escort of the breach of blackout procedures by the *Cedar Creek.*

The commodore waited until daylight to signal his demand for an explanation. The signal was the first Captain Svenson had heard of the matter. He was not pleased. He immediately summoned the gunnery officer and demanded an explanation. When the ensign admitted reluctantly that he had heard about it, Captain Svenson gave him the privilege of explaining to the commodore.

The ensign reported to the commodore by signal and was told that if such a lapse occurred again, both he and the gunners would answer personally to the Commander, North Atlantic Fleet, when they got back to the United States.

A seasoned officer would have let the matter end there, but the ensign was young and concerned about his record, so he signaled back that it was not a gunner but a monkey that had turned on the light.

The commodore, by now working up a full-blown rage, replied that the ensign could call his crew members whatever he liked—monkeys, baboons, or apes—but, by God, they better keep that light out!

Captain Svenson rolled his eyes and left the ensign on the signal bridge. The signalman had to bite his cheeks to keep from grinning.

Foolishly, the Ensign sent a more complete report, leaving no room for misunderstanding: it was indeed a real monkey, genus Callithrichidae, that had done the deed.

Near apoplexy, the commodore replied: "Upon arrival continental U.S. one Ensign is going to look like a monkey's ass, genus Callithrichidae. Stop. If you reply to this signal, we are prepared to shoot."

Every crewman on every ship who could see the signals and read Morse code was in hysterics.

Thereafter, the gun crew removed the light bulbs from the tool room each evening. (With the port holes painted black, they needed the lights in the daytime.)

Whether or not Ensign Monkey's Ass ever learned the wisdom of not offering too much advice to his superiors was an amusing subject of conversation in the seaman's quarters for the rest of the voyage. As for the real monkey demon, it was decided that he would become a British subject, provided the *Cedar Creek* reached Scotland.

Scotland

Under attack warnings most of the way, Jac's convoy crossed to a point just north of Ireland without a loss, in part because of the terrible weather they encountered. This had improved to a reasonably tolerable level, nasty but tolerable. All they had to do now was round Northern Ireland, enter the North Channel between Ireland and Scotland, and head south into the Irish Sea and their assigned port on the River Clyde.

The convoy split into two groups to proceed down the North Channel. The *Cedar Creek* moved to the column on the left, headed for Glasgow, the ships in the right column were headed further south to Liverpool.

For the first time since they left Halifax, the crew began to relax. They were following another T-2 tanker, also headed for the River Clyde. Then without the slightest warning, a torpedo slammed into the bow of the tanker ahead between her number one and number two tanks. She was making eleven knots at the time her bow was ripped off. The exposed forward bulkheads were ruptured by the force of her headway against the sea. Her liquid cargo pouring out, her propeller still turning, she drove her bow under until half of her was down, the stern rising out of the sea. Jac and his men watched in horror as the tanker's crew leaped overboard, and the vessel itself rolled on her back like a harpooned whale. There was no fire, probably because her cargo was kerosene and because her ruptured bow went under so quickly.

The *Cedar Creek* held her speed and station, moving through the sheen of kerosene spreading rapidly over the water. Her crew knew if they took a hit, any hit, they would not be so lucky. They were carrying gasoline.

Jac looked down at the men in the water, their eyes burning from the kerosene, their bodies freezing in the ice-cold water. He recognized one of them. Yet, they were lucky, for there were many escort vessels in the North Channel area, supplemented by fishing boats and coastal supply vessels, all rushing to aid the stricken ship and her crew.

The sinking was an example of the skill, determination, and daring of the U-boat skippers. Under the most protection the convoy had received on the entire voyage, a submarine had sneaked in and made a prize kill within sight of land. And, Jac realized, within five hundred yards of his own ship. Ironically, the tanker, with only her stern visible, refused to sink and had to be finished off by the guns of her own escorts.

The crew of the *Cedar Creek* had had a ringside seat to the entire episode. It could be their ship next time or the next. But for the moment there was nothing to do but continue on to their anchorage.

The *Cedar Creek* reached the Firth of Clyde and turned toward Glasgow. They put in at Gare Loch, overcrowded with ships waiting for a turn at the unloading facilities along the Clyde. It was the same at all the ports of the British Isles, where the Allies were stockpiling supplies in anticipation of D-Day. Normally it would take twenty hours or so to empty the tanker, but the *Cedar Creek* had to wait for ten days before the crowded port was ready to start unloading.

The crew didn't mind. It meant welcome days ashore, a chance to shed the stress of war at sea. It meant rollicking tours of pubs and honkytonks, the company of women, the sight of green grass and trees, the feel of solid earth beneath one's feet, and for some—perhaps when no one was watching—it meant a quiet visit to a church.

The citizens of Glasgow had little left. They had been at war for four years by now. Food was scarce, shops had very little to sell, gasoline was in such short supply that almost no one traveled by private automobile. Many of the children were hungry, there was no milk. Women had no stockings, no lipstick. Air raids had become a routine part of their lives, treated more as a nuisance than a deadly threat. But Glaswegians were friendly to the Americans. They knew that the convoys meant their survival, and they knew the price was being paid by the men who sailed them.

At home in Biloxi, Jac had made several friends among the British sailors who had been entertained by his family. One of them lived not far from Glasgow near the small town of Kirkintilloch. The boy's father worked in a coal mine. Smith took a day to go and see the family, as he had promised. He rode a bus as far as it went and walked the rest of the way. It was cold and windy. On the sunny sides of the hills there was some greenery among the brown grasses, and here and there were flocks of sheep. The sky was smeared with wind-blown clouds as if an artist had whisked white paint across blue canvas. It was a crisp day, a good day for a young man to be alive.

When he reached the cottage, his friend's family opened their arms to him. There was a language problem. Jac spoke English with a Southern accent, they with a Scots brogue. But hot tea and scones and a warm welcome was communication enough. His Royal Navy friend, Jac learned, was somewhere in the Mediterranean, trying to stop the flow of supplies to the Germans in North Africa.

He would later visit the families of other British friends, always remembering to take along something from the ship's stores—powdered milk, perhaps a little bacon, jam, American cigarettes (which had great value in wartime Britain and could be traded for almost anything). In the best of times, the British produced only about 30 percent of the food they consumed. In 1943, with the U-boat blockade cutting down on normal imports, basic food stuffs were tightly rationed and luxuries rare. Many an American merchant ship, before embarking on the return trip, would empty spare food stores at dockside, saving only what her cook felt was sufficient for the trip. Needless to say, there was always a crowd lining the docks to wish them safe voyage home—a crowd made up of pretty girls, children, families of friends, pub keepers, little old ladies, air raid wardens, all the types likely to be befriended by American seamen, young and old, who went ashore in wartime Britain.

Relieved of her liquid cargo, *Cedar Creek* moved down the Clyde and north to Loch Ewe to wait for a convoy to assemble. There in the sheltered waters Jac saw hundreds of seals, the first time he had seen these sleek creatures outside

Audubon Zoo in New Orleans. These were the mystic gray seals with human like faces, about whom the Scots, the Irish, and the Scandinavians told many legends. Perhaps they were a good omen for the voyages to come.

It was the end of January by then. The enemy left them alone on the return voyage, so there was nothing to worry about except huge seas, ice, and howling winds.

Old Hand

Back to the States, they remained barely long enough for the crew to go ashore, phone home, and let off a little steam. Then, her tanks filled again with gasoline, the *Cedar Creek* once more journeyed to Canada, took her place in a convoy, and faced the cold misery of the icy seas of February. This time ships were lost, but *Cedar Creek* made her way safely to Britain. Her crew considered her a lucky ship. She had the right joss, as old China hands would say.

The threat of dying hard was ever present, but the members of her crew were veterans now. They knew what to expect, how bad it could get. They worried less about measuring up and more about getting the job done.

Once again there were unintended moments of comedy to relieve the strain. This time the joke was on Jac.

Somewhere on shore he had acquired—quite innocently, he claimed—a terrible itching in his private parts. He was still a shy young man with very little knowledge of worldly ways, so he was all the more concerned when the itching did not go away. Fearing he had something awful, like maybe even leprosy, he confided in an older member of the crew. This man immediately stripped him down, and after a cursory examination called in a friend for a second opinion. They came to the unanimous conclusion that Boatswain Smith had a roaring infestation of *Phthirius pubis,* known in some circles as *crabs.*

Jac was appalled. He had led a rather chaste young life, under the influence of his puritanical grandfather, a stern man of the cloth, and he had never even heard of such pests. The men explained to him about crab lice.

"Well, what do I do to get rid of them? They're driving me crazy."

"Now, Jac, my boy," said one of the practitioners, "this calls for immediate action. We don't want the whole ship infested, do we?"

"What kind of action?"

"Very simple, very quick—an old sailors' remedy," said one.

"Yeah, nothing to it really," his partner agreed.

They took him to the engine room paint locker and told him to strip to the skin. His clothes were immediately soaked with turpentine. Then they dipped cotton wadding in turpentine and proceeded to saturate the affected areas. Jac had had turpentine on his hands many times with no noticeable effect, so he did not object. But he was startled when, the job done, his buddies leaped out of the compartment, and locked the door behind them.

Suddenly his private parts, fore and aft, leaped into flame. The words to a country song flashed through his mind:

The old tom cat was doing mighty fine,
Till they dipped his tail in the turpentine.
He's a moving on . . . he'll soon be gone.

Jac was moving too, only there was no place for him to go. The burning sensation had taken complete control of his mind and body, and it was demanding that he take some remedial action fast—like use of a fire hose. But there wasn't even a rag available. No amount of screaming, begging, threatening, cursing, and banging on the steel door could persuade his companions to let him out until enough time had passed.

After fifteen minutes, they decided the infestation must be over and unlocked the door. He would have taken a swing at them but for his haste to reach a source of soap and water. Up the ladder, down the companion way, through the galley—to the great amusement of a startled group of coffee drinkers—and finally to the shower, streaked a naked, rocket-powered boatswain. When the fresh gush of water poured over him, he discovered he was not mortally wounded. Blistered a little maybe, but totally louse free.

Jac was more worldly thereafter, but he tolerated badly the remarks he got when he showed up at meals with a pillow to sit on. It was days before he could put the incident—behind him.

On another occasion, cursing, which was not unknown aboardship even at uneventful times, was lifted to the paint-peeling level. It happened on a nasty night during a call to general quarters.

The *Cedar Creek* was blessed by having the company's senior radio operator on board, while at the same time cursed by the man's eccentricities, in particular his propensity toward finicky grouchiness. His cabin was organized with an almost religious devotion to neatness, everything clean, everything in its place. No one who visited his cabin dared touch, much less move, any item. The most prominent belonging was Sparks's wooden leg, set out in its place of honor.

The leg caused the radio operator a minimum of inconvenience. He could manage on the rolling deck of a ship about as well as anyone with two good legs. But he took it off the minute he was off duty and placed it at the foot of his couch, where it remained until he was ready to go on duty again.

Sparks's routine never varied. When he got off duty late in the evening, he would fix a cup of coffee in the galley, go to his cabin, light up a strong cigar, sit down on the couch, and take off his leg, carefully placing it in exactly the same position on the end of the couch, where it would remain during the night. After savoring the coffee and cigar, he would take a shower and go to bed.

A visitor could sit on the couch, but woe to the one who touched that leg!

The radio had to be manned twenty-four hours a day, so every ship had two radiomen to share the duties. It was customary for them to share the cabin next to the radio room as well. On this voyage First Sparks was assisted by a brand new young Second Sparks. Being fresh out of school, Second Sparks was a likable, fun-loving sort, who didn't take things seriously. He even looked lightly upon the fixed habits of his senior as an example of what too many years at sea could do to someone.

Precautions against discovery and attack were taken seriously by all on board. Every compartment on the ship was blacked out. Although portholes were painted black, they were sometimes opened at night for ventilation, but only after all lights in the room were out. Therefore, if a man came off duty late at night, he never turned on a light in his cabin until he checked to see if his roommate had opened a port-hole. Another rule was that each man had to carry a life jacket with him to his duty station. This was the rule that caused all the trouble. Because the radiomen's cabin was so close to their duty station, young Second Sparks seldom bothered to take his life jacket to the radio room.

One night about 2 a.m., without warning, a torpedo hit a ship next to the *Cedar Creek*. All manner of alarms went off. Second Sparks, who was on duty, didn't need reminding that this was the real thing. He went flying from the radio room into his cabin next door, grabbed his life jacket, then dashed back to his duty station. However, in diving through the dark room to get his jacket, he knocked First Sparks wooden leg off the couch. It flew across the room and lodged under the desk.

First Sparks was a deep sleeper, but finally the alarm got his attention. Still in darkness, he leaped out of bed on his one leg and grabbed for his artificial one, which wasn't there. With the alarm bell ringing off the wall, he went leaping about in the dark on one leg, cursing the air purple, trying to get into his zoot suit. When off duty, crewmen were supposed to re-port to their lifeboat stations when the alarm sounded. It was not long before those on deck saw a cursing, hopping, one-legged apparition, supporting himself with the rail. First Sparks was shouting a continuous string of invectives: "The damn son and heir of a mongrel bitch with goat turds for brains who's hidden my leg is going to be a eunuch by sun up!"

The men watching his approach forgot about the threat of attack, amazed at the speed, method of locomotion, and vociferous rage of this vision. The empty leg of his zoot suit flopped out behind him after every hop, looking like the tail of a kangaroo, and the string of obscenities spouting from him filled them with awe.

Jac ordered himself not to laugh—a man, handicapped by having only one leg, struggling along the deck of a ship in rough seas while under submarine attack, should not be considered funny. But he found himself helplessly disobeying his own orders. Soon half the crew was similarly demoralized.

At the time, no one, including Second Sparks, knew what had happened to the artificial leg. Only later, after the leg was found under the desk, did the young radio operator bravely—if sheepishly—suggest that perhaps in his haste to retrieve his lifejacket he might have knocked the leg flying. First Sparks, barely restrained from killing his assistant, finally calmed down and stopped cussing. And the affair was considered closed.

But Second Sparks was thereafter a changed man. He carried his life jacket with him at all times and explained to anyone who would listen that he did not deliberately hide his partner's wooden leg. (He went on to become a First Sparks himself.)

After once more emptying a load of gasoline in Scotland, the *Cedar Creek* joined a convoy headed for New York. A tanker, she was ballasted down low with her tanks filled with water. The poor general cargo ships returning empty, even with rock ballast, rode high and miserable in the rolling mountainous seas. The enemy submarines frequently chose not to waste one of their precious torpedoes on an empty ship, but they would try for a tanker any time they could get a shot at one. The tankers carried the heart's blood of the Allied war effort, and the enemy knew it.

Each trip ships were lost from the convoy, but the *Cedar Creek* always made port without taking a direct hit. That does not mean that her crew was not scarred by the experience. Homeward bound on one crossing, Jac saw a scene that still haunts his darkest dreams. On a cold day with relatively easy seas, the lookout spied a line of life jackets off the port bow, and the captain altered course slightly to bring them close aboard. Jac stepped to the rail and looked down. There was a chain of eight life vests tied together with rope—tied by men desperate to survive, men who did not want to be alone on the cold sea, men who believed their chances for rescue would be better if they could stay together. They were still together, skeletal bits and pieces of them hanging there in those life jackets, silently bobbing away into the oncoming darkness.

A Russian Captain

The *Cedar Creek* continued to make crossings carrying gasoline to Britain without serious mishap. Her crew came home unscarred on the outside, but from each crossing there were more visions of dying men and ships to crowd the deep black corners of their memories.

Even the enemy below was haunted by the horror of convoy battles of the North Atlantic as evidenced in the writings of one of them after the war. Lothar-Gunther Buchheim in his book, *U-Boat War,* wrote of a ship his sub had torpedoed on a night surface attack. He described what he saw from the bridge of his U-boat:

> All around the wreck, dark red flames rise straight off the water—the antagonistic elements of water and fire combine. The sea is burning.
>
> Even the strongest swimmer meets with a ghastly end in such a hell—burned in the water, corroded by the oil, suffocated by the smoke, he dies a manifold death.

The stench of burning tankers filled the air . . . Anyone signing up aboard a tanker crosses the threshold of hell.

But on a cold night in March 1944 such thoughts were not present among the men of the tanker, *Cedar Creek,* as she passed from Lower Bay through the Narrows into Upper Bay, and the lights of Jersey City and Manhattan came into view. The city lights were a welcome sight. The *Cedar Creek* was eased into the Brooklyn shipyard where she was dwarfed alongside the once grand French liner *Normandie.* In the yard for conversion to a troop carrier, the beautiful ship had caught fire at her berth in February of 1942 and capsized from the weight of the water pumped into her to extinguish the fire. Now, after two years of salvage work, her gutted hulk was afloat. The crew of the *Cedar Creek* was awed by her size. They began counting her portholes but gave up after tallying more than a thousand.(*Normandie* would never sail again. She was towed to a scrap yard after the war.)

But more cheerful sights were at hand for a sea-weary crew. There was time to go ashore, time for the bright lights of Broadway. Jac and a few friends rode the subway into Manhattan and had a seafood dinner at Toffenetti's. The United Seaman's Club was just around the corner. This was a substitute for the various USO canteens, which did not admit merchant seamen because they were not part of the armed forces. But Broadway personalities and starlets often entertained at the Seaman's Club in New York, and show tickets were given away.

Jac used a phone at the club to call home: "Yes, Mom, I'm fine, just fine. Sure, Dad, it's a little rough at times, but nothing to worry about."

What else could he tell them? That he had seen men die, burned or frozen, that ships disappeared in flame, that God only knew when or if he would return home? That he was lonely and often afraid? Of course not. It was enough just to hear each other's voices.

At the Seaman's Club a cheerful little lady gave away show tickets, a comedy with Milton Berle and Sophie Tucker. Jac and a few friends decided to go. The next night he saw a production of *The Merry Widow.* He had a box seat to that one, in fact the entire box. His buddies preferred burlesque. He thought the theater was a wonderful discovery. It made him forget the war for a couple of hours.

Afterward he walked around the theater district, watching the well-dressed crowds, listening to the laughter of reveling groups, noticing an occasional pretty girl. If there weren't so many uniforms in the crowds, you might not even know there was a war, he thought. He was hungry, but he didn't think he would feel comfortable with the well-dressed after-theater crowd at a big-city restaurant. Instead he bought a hot dog and a beer and took the subway to Brooklyn. From the subway station, Jac walked alone down long blocks of warehouses to the shipyard where the *Cedar Creek* was docked.

The next morning a Russian naval captain came aboard. The first officer asked Smith to give the visitor, who could speak a little English, a tour of the ship. The Russian wanted to see the entire vessel, bow to stern, ammo storage to paint locker, engine room to bridge. Jac wondered just what was going on.

Lend-Lease to Russia was going on. The *Cedar Creek* was to have a new owner, eventually a new name. There was one more thing. The Russian captain asked for three volunteers to help deliver the ship to the Soviet Union: Jac, the assistant engineer, and an AB.

Captain Svenson explained: The Russians were inexperienced with turbo-electric power systems. The first assistant engineer was thoroughly familiar with all the ship's power systems; moreover, he could speak some Ukrainian. Jac knew every piece of machinery and equipment on deck, and the AB (able bodied seaman) would assist him in training the Russian crew during the voyage.

The Americans talked it over among themselves. They knew the trip to Russia would be a tough one—the Murmansk Run was almost legendary for its danger and difficulties. They went to their company office, the Marine Transport Line, located near Wall Street on Broadway. Company spokesmen told the men that they were cleared to go if they so desired and that, if they chose to go, the Russians had agreed to pay them in American dollars at their usual rates plus a bonus.

There was a war on, their gear was already on board, they knew the ship. They volunteered.

The crew that came aboard the next morning numbered only slightly more than half the normal number of crewmen considered standard for a T-2 tanker. Six of them were women. They were all Soviet navy.

The captain hired a river pilot and immediately took the ship on a trial run up the Hudson River. There were no enemy submarines up the Hudson River, and the river pilot could handle the bridge while the captain familiarized himself with the ship and encouraged his crew to be quick learners. Each would have to do the work of two on the voyage home. They steamed to Poughkeepsie and back before the captain was satisfied. He made sure that each member of his crew knew that the three Americans were on board to train them—and that they would learn, or else. He also did something that astounded the pilot. After his tour of the ship, he returned to the bridge, and like a kid with a new toy he blew the ship's whistle, not once, but repeatedly. He would blow the whistle and laugh. The agitated pilot, afraid the unusual signals would confuse every vessel on the river, at last got across to the captain that one didn't play with the whistle of a 600-foot ship while navigating a channel.

The first assistant engineer was known to Jac as Firsty. Nicknames were common aboardship. Some men were known by no other name. On a merchant ship a man's past, family, and background were considered private information, and no one pried. The AB was George Borrkle. He had been a member of Jac's deck crew and was a good man.

The *Cedar Creek* made a few minor repairs at the shipyard. Then, fit and ready, she began loading her cargo for the voyage. This would be a very special convoy.

The Murmansk Run

By early 1943, the run to the northern Russian ports of Murmansk and Archangel (Arkhangel'sk) had become so costly—out of fifty ships in one convoy, only sixteen survived—that they were stopped. Stalin badgered the Allies unceasingly to resume them.

There were only two other supply routes to Russia. One was through the eastern port of Vladivostok northeast of Korea, behind the main Japanese island of Honshu. Because the Soviet Union was not at war with Japan, only Russian ships, which were in very short supply, could get to Vladivostok. The other supply route was via the Persian Gulf to Iran, and then by truck to Russia. Both routes were almost twice as far by sea as Murmansk, and both were sharply restricted by long slow railway hauls across Russia. Therefore, the Murmansk Run through the Arctic Ocean had the greatest potential capacity for supplying the Russians. The Allies needed Russia to continue to fight the Nazis on the Eastern front. The convoys were resumed in September 1943.

Improved escort tactics using high frequency direction-finding gear (HF/DF), affectionately called Huff Duff, and radar were beginning to take their toll on submarines. However, the Nazis were acutely aware that the Murmansk–Archangel convoys represented Russia's lifeline. They were determined to cut it.

Every merchant ship assigned to the Murmansk Run was loaded to the maximum, sometimes beyond. Losses were expected. Those ships that got through had to deliver all the goods they could carry.

Cedar Creek was loaded with high-test aviation gasoline. Then she was moved to a dock equipped with huge cranes, which lifted four heavy steam locomotives onto specially prepared cradles, two forward, two aft, all of which were lashed and welded securely to the deck. After that, the remaining deck space was loaded with aircraft, their wings and engines removed, crated and lashed to the ship. Jac was responsible for the deck and everything on it. Painstakingly he checked the lashings and fittings of the deck cargo to insure that all was secure, and then checked them again. The last thing he wanted, on a ship carrying 90,000 barrels of aviation gasoline, was for one of those ponderous behemoths to break loose in a stormy sea. He had never seen—or even heard of—a tanker being so heavily loaded. He hoped that the men who had come up with the loading plan knew what they were doing.

Once more through the Narrows, *Cedar Creek* left New York behind and joined a small convoy. It was late April, 1944. They hurried up the East Coast to Halifax, where, with as much secrecy and caution as possible, a convoy to Russia was being hastily assembled. Jac didn't like the way the heavily loaded *Cedar Creek* had wallowed and rolled en route, even in moderate seas. It was nothing alarming, but, still, how would the tanker respond when it had to confront the wild North Atlantic?

No time for going ashore this trip. Assembled in the convoy were American and British ships, some free Norwegian ships which had escaped from Norway to join the Allies, and a few Russians. One of the latter was the newly acquired T-2 tanker with three American volunteers among its crew, who had learned during the short cruise from New York that, whatever else happened, they would be eating a lot of potatoes and cabbage on their voyage to Russia.

On a cold and windy day at the opening of May, Jac sent a detail forward to man the anchor windlass. The voyage had begun. From Halifax the convoy—some fifty ships strong—silently passed Cape Race and entered the storm belt between Newfoundland and Cape Farewell, Greenland. Jac had passed this way before and knew what to expect: screaming winds, giant waves, sleet, rain, snow flurries, gray skies day after day after day. At times the fog would be so thick that, from the bridge, Jac could not see the bow.

Beyond Cape Farewell they swung in an arc that would place them under the protection of long-range aircraft from Iceland—B-24s and B-17s—when weather permitted. Then on to northern Scotland on the first leg toward Russia.

The *Cedar Creek* was burdened in a way her designers had not imagined. In heavy seas, the weight of her massive deck cargo caused her to corkscrew beyond anything Jac had seen before. Her decks awash, she would roll to one side and pause there—moaning, shaking, and shuddering from stem to stern—before slowly, reluctantly, bringing herself upright to begin a roll to the other side. And all the while pitching— bow down and stern high, then reverse—so that the tanker was constantly worked by the seas. A fact that Jac kept to himself, but could not put from his mind, was that in these same waters, under these same conditions, another heavily laden ship, commanded by the convoy's commodore, had capsized without warning. There had been no survivors.

The crew's quarters on a T-2 were considered excellent by the standards of the day, roomy and well-furnished, but in those seas there was no comfort aboard any ship. A topside trip from the deck house aft, where most of the crew lived, to the bridge amidships was a wild and hazardous dash. Even the elevated catwalks were often awash. Trying to reach the forecastle on the bow—a trip the lookouts and gun crews had to make every four hours when the watch changed—was even more of a thrill, one that left men bashed and bruised and soaked. Standing by the lifeboats could be a life-threatening assignment.

Still, experiences aboard the tanker were nothing compared to the fun had by the men who manned the escort and rescue vessels. These were smaller ships, destroyers, destroyer escorts, corvettes, and ocean-going tugs, supplied by the British and American navies and by the Coast Guard. Men aboard them felt as though they were riding the agitator in a washing machine. They had to hang on to keep from being flung about their duty stations. Minor injuries occurred daily, broken bones were not uncommon. Many stood their watches holding a bucket in which to throw up, and not apologizing for their seasickness. Men off duty, trying to sleep, were thrown out of their bunks. If you wanted to eat, and the cook could keep his fire lighted, you first had to capture and hold your plate of food.

All of this occurred under the constant strain and fear of submarine attack. The convoy would get a warning: An escort had picked up a sub contact. Everyone aboardship would get the word. Fear. Some men showed it, some didn't, but everyone shared it. Perhaps there were some on board who had survived sinkings on earlier voyages. One might put a hand on the shoulder of a young seaman and say, "Ease up a little. I've been through it, and I came out all right"—and then turn away wondering if, in truth, he could go through it again. There had been an easing of sub attacks in early 1943 as new antisubmarine tactics proved successful. But Germany, whose shipyards were producing a sub a day, gained the U-boat fleet Admiral Doenitz needed for a new Atlantic offensive. Merchant ship losses in 1943 climbed to those of 1942. But submarines would not be the main worry of this convoy.

Jac and George Borrkle trained the Russians on the deck machinery, lifeboat davits, and the guns. They didn't have to stand regular watches, so they spent a lot of time on the bridge with the captain or checking their ship, undermanned, overloaded, and vulnerable.

Although they had a number of U-boat warnings during the crossing, they suffered no torpedoings. Perhaps the German wolf packs tracking them already knew where they were headed and what was planned for them. The convoy made Loch Ewe in northern Scotland and stayed just one day, long enough to repair minor damage from the stormy crossing and inspect and tighten deck-cargo lashings. Then they sailed past the Shetland Islands and set a course that would take them through the Norwegian Sea into the Arctic Circle, then around North Cape into the Barents Sea and northern Russia. The course, three hundred miles offshore, paralleled the long western coastline of Norway—a Norway occupied by Germany.

Jac remembers, "The bad part began there." His face grew troubled as he told the story. "The seas were running high and there was pack ice in the water, even though it was May, but the sky was clear for flying." And the planes came. They came from Stavanger and Bergen, Trondheim and Levanger, Narvik and Hammerfest. They came with black crosses on their wings. From their bellies poured bombs and torpedoes. The ships steered a course as far offshore as the ice would allow, but the planes found them. Ahead of the slow-plodding ships, they dropped mines. Then they flew away and came back by night, the pale Arctic sun barely dipped below the horizon.

There were twin-engined Messerschmitt Bf 110-Gs, Heinkel 111 He-torpedo bombers, twin-engined Junkers and Stuka dive bombers. They came for six straight days and nights.

The ships fought off some of the attackers. Gun crews fired their 20 mm machine guns until the barrels almost melted. Some cargo ships fired all their ammunition, and then the crews went down into the holds, broke into ammunition cargoes destined for Russia, and fired them. Planes went down, and ships were sunk, many ships.

The Russians on the *Cedar Creek* did their best. Shorthanded to begin with, they were pushed to the limits of endurance. The three Americans helped where they could— the engineer down below, and Jac and George Borrkle on deck keeping ammo coming to the gun crews. The captain zigzagged as wildly as he dared to avoid attacks.

Ships around them took hits. Some kept going. Others did not. An ammunition ship in the center of the convoy took a direct hit. Within a split second she disappeared. There was a blinding flash, a roar—and when the smoke cleared, there was only dust on the sea.

Bombs straddled the *Cedar Creek* repeatedly. Shrapnel littered her decks, and there were casualties, but she kept going. Her overworked Russian crew and the three American crewmen ate little and slept, if at all, at their duty stations.

A tanker two columns over took a hit. Like *Cedar Creek* she was carrying gasoline and exploded in a ball of flame that engulfed the entire ship in less than four minutes. Her only three survivors had been on the stern when the bomb hit forward. They jumped off the weather side of the stern, the only place around the ship where the sea wasn't on fire. There had been no time to lower lifeboats, but the falls to one burned through, and it dropped into the sea. The three survivors swam to the burning lifeboat, somehow helped one another to climb aboard, and put out the fire.

Another liberty ship, with hundreds of drums of gasoline lashed to her decks, burst into flames, then broke in half. One of her lifeboats, containing only a handful of survivors, was last seen helplessly drifting downwind into a blazing patch of sea.

Those who managed to reach lifeboats or made it to rafts cut away when there was no time to launch boats had a chance to survive. Those in the ice-filled water for more than a few minutes did not.

Sometimes a ship escaped without catching fire. Sometimes a crew fought a fire and won, and their ship steamed on. Crippled ships fell behind. Out of the protective concentrated fire of the convoy, they were easily finished off by the attackers.

From horizon to horizon Jac saw smoke from dying ships. He knew men were dying with them—by drowning, by freezing, by burning, from wounds. If they made it to a lifeboat, perhaps they would die from hunger or thirst or gangrene or exposure unless rescue arrived in time.

Beyond the Arctic Circle, even in May, survivors suffered from frostbite, especially those who spent time in the water. It was not unusual for rescue personnel to find survivors with gangrenous fingers and toes. Out of one group of 400 rescued seamen, many lost limbs from the cold. One survivor estimated that at least twenty of them had had both arms and legs amputated.

On the Murmansk Run everyone was a hero. John Creswell in his book, *Sea Warfare 1939–1945,* stated it well when he said, "It would be generally agreed that nowhere was courage shown under conditions of such prolonged strain, seemingly adverse odds, and intense climatic discomfort as on the convoy routes to North Russia."

Individual sacrifice was common. It is difficult, often impossible to launch lifeboats safely while a ship is underway. When an order was given to abandon ship, the "black gang"—if they were still alive—would try to shut the engines down and halt the propellers, so the ship could lose way and launch her boats. Then, if they could find their way out of the engine room—sometimes flooded, sometimes filled with smoke, steam, fire, often in total darkness—they would race to reach an open deck and a chance to live. One naval armed guard crew, ordered to abandon ship, was seen still firing their guns as the ship slipped under. On another ship two men were isolated from the lifeboats by fire. One of them was an old salt (you do not refer to any man at sea as elderly) who took off his life vest and gave it to the young man with him who had none. On one tanker an assistant engineer ran down a deck of flaming oil to reach a fire-suppression valve and open it. He himself was badly burned, but his action made possible the launching of lifeboats and saved his fellow crewmen. On another occasion, with the sea on fire, a boatswain cut loose a raft, swam to it through the flames, and shouted encouragement to his terrified fellow crew members to follow him. Three times he dived back into the burning sea to drag seaman through the last few feet of flames to the raft. Though everyone suffered burns, they were all rescued and survived.

And still the planes came.

The rescue vessels gathered as many survivors as they could. In heavy seas some rigged nets on outriggers in an attempt to scoop up men in the water. Crew members on board risked their lives climbing down to aid men too numb to climb or even hold onto the nets. Some survivors in lifeboats made it to the shores of Norway. Most were placed in labor prison camps by the Germans. A fortunate few found their way into the hands of the Norwegian resistance forces.

Ironically, the Germans were occasionally chivalrous during the battles of the Murmansk Run. Once a German air-sea rescue plane risked landing to pick up over a dozen survivors from an isolated lifeboat in the Norwegian Sea. On another occasion a U-boat surfaced beside a lifeboat. Its skipper gave the survivors what they needed most: a compass, chart, their position and course to nearest land. He also gave them biscuits, cigarettes, water, and blankets.

This captain had ignored standing orders of U-boat operations not to surface for survivors, which had been issued after an unfortunate mishap earlier in the war. A German U-boat had surfaced to pick up survivors, because its skipper had realized that many of them were civilian passengers, too many for the available number of lifeboats on the sinking merchant vessel. With over thirty survivors on the submarine's deck and many more in the water around it, the sub came under direct attack from an American B-24. A young lieutenant flying on submarine patrol had picked up the ship's SOS, and as soon as he sighted the surfaced U-boat, he made an immediate attack, dropping two depth charges. The explosions straddled the sub, which made a crash dive to escape. Many of the survivors in the water were killed, and those on the sub's deck were either drowned or scattered in the sea without aid.

Under convoy rules no merchant ship could stop for survivors. To do so would risk the lives of the crew, the ship, and ten thousand tons of cargo. A ship dead in the water picking up survivors was a target an enemy couldn't miss. Jac Smith and the others fighting to save their ships, themselves, and each other remember the agony of having to leave others behind, hoping a rescue vessel would find them. From the decks they looked down into the drifting lifeboats at faces they can never forget, faces black with oil, faces in pain, cold faces, determined faces, hopeless faces, and sometimes, faces that smiled as if to say, "I'm all right, mate." One captain passing nearby looked down at the men in a lifeboat and saw such a face. With heart-stopping recognition, he saw his son smile up at him and wave. He had to keep his ship moving. With a salute and a father's prayer he watched the lifeboat quickly pass astern. It was the last time he ever saw his son.

The merchant ships steamed relentlessly on, past the rafts, past the lifeboats, past floating bodies turned to blue chunks of ice, or charred black by flaming oil.

Molotovsk

Jac's convoy, what was left of it, stayed far out toward Bear Island, carving as wide a path around the tip of Norway as the Arctic pack ice would allow, until it arrived off Murmansk, well inside the Arctic Circle and only fifty-five miles from German-occupied territory. Far offshore the crew of the *Cedar Creek* could see the barrage balloons that marked the harbor, tethered all over the port. The blimps were there to discourage low-flying enemy aircraft, but air raids occurred daily nonetheless. German aircraft, in anticipation of the arrival of the convoy, had dropped mines at all the harbor approaches. Entering Murmansk harbor was extremely hazardous.

The Russian captain of the *Cedar Creek* made the decision to proceed toward Archangel instead. That was a gamble, too, because the entrance to the White Sea is closed by pack ice except for the short spring and summer, opening sometime in May and closing again in September. But it was a matter of weighing one danger against another.

The *Cedar Creek* proceeded east along the Kola Peninsula and turned south, easing slowly through the ice-crowded, barely passable entrance to the White Sea. After a long and arduous passage, they finally arrived at what Jac thought was Archangel. In fact Archangel's harbor was not deep enough to accommodate a fully loaded tanker. They had reached Molotovsk (now called Severodvinsk) across the Dviña delta from Archangel. (Until recently, Jac never knew he was not in Archangel.)

Archangel is just 150 miles south of the Arctic circle and only fifty miles south of 65 degrees latitude, the line across the north of Russia that delineates the southern border of Central and Eastern Siberia. Murmansk is well above this line.

There the three Americans were paid off—in Russian rubles. They had been promised pay in American dollars, because rubles were worthless outside Russia. They tried to refuse to accept the money. They protested, they reasoned, they demanded, but what they got was a basketful of rubles and the address of an office in town where, they were told, they could register their problems.

Jac was mad as hell. What could he do with rubles? He figured he had more than earned his pay, and he wanted the money he had been promised in spendable American dollars. He tried to see the captain. He saw only the pay officer, who was backed up by a pair of armed Russian sailors. Jac picked up his seabag and led Firsty and Borrkle into what he thought was downtown Archangel.

It was mostly wooden buildings with a few masonry structures here and there. The streets appeared to be dirt covered with muddy black snow, which crunched under their feet. White snow still lay on the roofs of the buildings and houses, and melting icicles hung from eaves. Spring has a very hard time replacing winter in northernmost Russia. In the shadows, windowpanes were frosted over, and in the sunlight many were fogged from the inside. The people Jac saw on the street were mostly old. They took no notice of the American seamen who were dressed much the way they were themselves except perhaps for Jac's great sheepskin coat. The Russian citizens wore heavy wool coats. A few wore coats of fur similar to those of Eskimos.

The address Jac had been given turned out to be that of the local NKVD (forerunner of today's KGB), which dealt with all matters concerning foreigners. It was a masonry building with sturdy double wooden doors. They entered a hallway about eight feet wide. Ten or so feet down the hall on the left, a door opened into a long room with wooden benches along each side. One man sat on the bench near the door. A single light fixture, a light bulb with a frosted shade, hung by its cord from the ceiling. The wall at the far end of the room had an open door, flanked by counters topped by what looked like boarded-up tellers' windows. Beyond the door they could see a small room with a desk, behind which sat a dour-faced man in some sort of official-looking uniform. The three Americans entered the room and stood before the desk. The Russian looked up from his papers, said something in Russian that sounded like "Well, what do you want?"

Jac was young and mad, and didn't give a damn who he was talking to. (Besides, he had no idea this was the NKVD, which he had never heard of anyway.) He tried to explain the problems, but the official either didn't understand English, or pretended he didn't. The man sitting on the bench in the anteroom got up and entered the smaller office. He explained that he did speak English, said he was a newspaper reporter, and offered to translate for them.

Boatswain Smith explained that he had helped bring a supply ship to Russia, that there had been fifty ships in the convoy, many of which had been lost. In fact, he himself had seen at least eleven of them sunk. (The convoy had in fact lost almost one ship out of three.) He told them that the three Americans on the *Cedar Creek* had been promised that their pay would be in American dollars, and that there were supposed to be arrangements for their transportation back to the United States.

Whether or not there was a real misunderstanding, or the Russian captain decided to keep the American dollars for himself—or the NKVD got a cut of what at the time was a significant amount of American money, or whether there was never any intention of paying American dollars—will never be known. The uniformed official denied any knowledge of the pay problem. In fact, he denied any knowledge of Americans serving on a Russian ship. He also denied having knowledge of any arrangements for them to be returned to England, America, or anywhere else by ship. The three American seamen protested even louder. The result was that the Russian official waved them out of the room and returned to his paper work.

The reporter suggested they get a room at a hotel down the street and work things out tomorrow. He also said that if they waited at the corner two blocks away, about seven o'clock that night, a truck would pick them up and carry them to a party to celebrate the arrival of the convoy. Jac thanked him. He then led his group back to the *Cedar Creek* to get her captain. When he arrived, the letters "Cedar Creek" were already being painted over in preparation for lettering on her new Russian name. (Jac never knew her Russian name, *Taganrog*, for a seaport city at the mouth of the Donets, until that fact came to light during this writing.) The captain was gone. That left the hotel.

It was a two-story heavy wooden structure, drab, short on plumbing, but friendly enough compared to the NKVD office. The three Americans entered the front door. Inside was a lobby sparsely furnished with a few chairs and a stove, plus, on the right side, an area with a lower ceiling supported by square wooden posts, which was furnished with a few tables and chairs and another stove. Two men sat at one of the tables, a bottle of vodka and two glasses between them. Directly in front of them opposite the front door was a wooden stairway and to its left a wall across the corner of the room. This wall sported a grilled window, like a bank teller's, behind which a man looked curiously at them. The room was lighted by fixtures hanging by their cords from the ceiling, their naked light bulbs covered by frosted-glass shades.

Jac walked over to the window and said they wanted three rooms. Nothing. Then he made a pillow out of his hands and laid his head on them indicating sleep, pointed to the other two Americans, and held up three fingers. The man handed them a register to sign and motioned that he wanted their passports by holding up what must have been his own ID book. They did as he asked. Then each took out a pocketful of rubles. The clerk took an equal amount from each of them, disappeared, reappeared, and led them up the worn wooden stairs and down a bare, dimly lighted hallway. The hall had perhaps six or eight rooms on each side and ended at a window. They were given the third, fourth, and fifth rooms on the right side.

Jac walked into his room and dropped his seabag on the wooden floor. On one side there was a plain wooden chair, on the other a washstand with an enameled metal pitcher, wash bowl, and continuous towel hanging on a wooden roller rod. The towel "loop" hung about three feet down the wall. Between the washstand and the bed there was a thunder mug—a chamber pot, like the ones Jac had seen on his grandmother's farm. The plain wooden three-quarter bed was covered by a heavy patchwork quilt and under that by sheets of a woven material that reminded Jac of dish towels. The window had curtains made of the same material. He could see the side street through the streaked window glass. Sitting on the bed, he felt more alone than he ever had in his life.

Jac made an assessment of his situation. He was in Russia at the edge of the Arctic Circle, had no American money, was not at the port where he had been expected, didn't know how he was going to get to Murmansk, much less to England or America. Except for his two shipmates, he had not seen any other Americans. He didn't know if there was an American representative in the whole place. (There was an American naval office in both Molotovsk and Archangel, but no one had ever bothered to tell the three merchant seaman—on their first trip to Russia—anything about that. After all, they weren't Navy, they were civilians.) Then he remembered the party. That would be better than staying in a bleak, lonely hotel room. He was alive, he had survived, he would sort out his problems in the morning. Tonight there would be music, and girls—Russian girls, but girls nonetheless—and maybe a beer or two. Jac Smith was not quite twenty years old.

He rousted out his two shipmates. Early May or not, the evening was cold, the snow and ice not giving up easily; what melted in the thin Arctic sunshine refroze after sundown. Where there was no traffic, streets were filled with crunchy mush or solid patches of ice. Jac dressed in three pairs of pants, three shirts, and his heavy sheepskin coat. The three Americans waited at the appointed corner for the promised transportation to the party. A short while later an army truck arrived, picked them up, and drove several miles out of town to some kind of Russian camp. The party was held in a large wooden building that looked like a dining hall.

Inside, benches and tables lined the walls, and along the wall opposite the front door, a band was playing. It turned out to be a "bring your own" party, but that turned out to be no problem. The Americans were offered straight vodka by those sitting around them. One long swig of raw vodka was enough for Jac; it stoked his boiler and burned its way from his throat to his toes. He looked around for some beer but didn't find any. There was no food either. It seemed these Russians were serious party people.

Jac's little group seemed to be the only foreigners there, as far as he could determine. Some of the Russians, both men and women, were in uniform, but most wore civilian dress. Then his attention turned to the music and the girls. At first the three young Americans held back a little, trying to pick out the prettiest among the girls. The first two Jac asked to dance politely refused. Then one of the Russians sitting near him pointed out a girl across the room, and she rose and followed him to the dance floor. Later others said yes to invitations from the Americans, and eventually it dawned on the three seamen that only certain girls would be allowed to dance with them. Some of the "allowed" ones were in uniform.

It didn't matter. The Russians were allies, weren't they? The seamen were glad to be ashore at a party with laughter and music, even if it was in Russia on a cold spring night with girls whose language they could not understand.

The evening seemed over too soon. The three Americans crawled into the back of a crowded army truck and were happily driven into town, humming Russian tunes. They got out on a corner a couple of blocks from the hotel and started down the street. Out of cigarettes, they decided to see if they could find a shop open where they could buy some and spend some of their useless rubles. No shops were open. In fact, it dawned on them that they were alone in the streets. By the time they gave up and started for the hotel, the time was twenty minutes after midnight—twenty minutes too late.

Twenty Minutes Too Late

They turned the corner and could see their hotel. That was when a police van pulled up, and they were ordered to get in the back. They asked why. The uniformed Russian policemen growled something at them which they could not understand, but it didn't sound friendly. Jac pointed at the hotel and using sign language tried to explain that they were going there to sleep. The policemen shoved them toward the back of the police truck. They shoved back. George was knocked to the ground, a cut on his head. They were hustled into the truck and taken to a place they had seen before—the NKVD office.

They were marched into the office, where their loud complaints were greeted by the same unsmiling official who had thrown them out of the office earlier. He was also irritated at being gotten out of bed. He looked at them and pronounced a single statement in clear English, "Curfew midnight!" It was by then 12:45.

"What curfew? We weren't told of any curfew."

The ignorance of foreign troublemakers was no concern of the Russian official. Besides, he had already had one run-in with these same foreign troublemakers. He gave a couple of orders to the armed policemen and waved his hand in dismissal. That didn't sound encouraging to Jac. One of the police left the room and returned a short while later followed by three sleepy, unhappy-looking armed soldiers. The interview was over.

As it turned out the trial was also over, the sentence given.

The three Americans expected to be escorted to their hotel or to pay a fine. Instead they were dragged, kicking and screaming, to a truck where they were invited, at the point of a submachine gun, to climb into the back. They were joined by the soldier with the gun. He motioned for them to sit forward on a bench just behind the cab and took a seat at the back of the truck, where he pulled down a torn canvas flap that loosely closed the back of the truck. Then he laid the submachine gun across his knees with its barrel pointed in the direction of his charges.

The truck jerked forward through its gears into high. It made several turns and then picked up speed, leaving the town behind. The three prisoners were not allowed to talk. The road got bumpier, but the truck did not slacken its pace. The three could hardly stay on their bench, much less get any sleep. It grew colder in the back of the truck. Jac was thankful he had worn so much clothing, especially his great sheepskin coat. As hour followed hour, they became hungry and thirsty, and they were desperately in need of relieving themselves. Sign language failed to move the guard. When they couldn't hold back any longer, they simply let go, and the urine, steaming in the cold air, streamed down the bed of the truck and drained away. The Americans were hideously embarrassed, but the guard showed no emotion at all.

Jac suspected that the soldier didn't like the ride anymore than they did. He probably blamed them for this unpleasant extra duty, too. When Jac pushed his sleeve back and looked at his watch, the soldier stirred as though his attention had finally been caught.

It was past six in the morning by the time they stopped. The sky seen through the torn flap was brightening, indicating that they had been traveling west. Jack did some hasty mental arithmetic. They had been driving at least thirty miles an hour for more than five and a half hours. They must be at least 150 miles west of where they had started. He was also sure they were in a great deal of trouble. Unless, he thought suddenly, they had been transported to Murmansk!

The flap covering the back of the truck was lifted, and they were ordered out. One thing was certain: they had traveled north as well as west. It was colder and there seemed to be more snow about. The soldier who had ridden with them relieved them of their watches before they climbed out. Then he jumped down from the back and motioned them forward. In the gray light of dawn, Jac could make out several buildings surrounded by barbed wire, gate houses, and armed guards. Wherever this was, it wasn't Murmansk.

The soldier turned the Americans over to the camp guards and climbed into the cab of the truck with his two comrades. The truck drove off through the gate and disappeared down the road, its tires throwing up mud mixed with snow.

The bewildered new arrivals were motioned to a small building, where they were each given a bowl, a spoon, and one thin blanket. Still not quite believing what was happening to them, they were taken to separate barrack buildings, each about fifteen feet by forty. Mushy snow was drifted all along the walls except in front of the door. Icicles hung down from the roofs, slowly melting as spring struggled to displace winter.

Jac walked to the entrance of his barracks followed by a guard. He clutched the blanket and the bowl and spoon in his arms as he might have clutched a lifejacket aboard a ship sinking beneath him. He was stunned. His mind kept trying to reject the reality of what was happening, but Jac knew it was no dream. He stopped in front of the door. The guard motioned for him to enter and walked away.

He opened the door. The stale odor of sour bedding and unwashed bodies filled his nostrils. Accustomed to the clean air of the sea, he was sickened by the miasma that came from the barracks. The place was heated by one wood-burning stove in the center and consequently nearly as cold as outdoors. As his eyes adjusted to the dim light from a single electric bulb hanging by a cord from the ceiling, he made out rows of crude bunks built four high against the walls, each one only twenty inches above the one below. Most of them were taken. Both men and women were housed in the building, looking exhausted, dirty, hungry, miserable. No one took much notice of him. They had seen new ones walk in and old ones carried out. He was just another new one.

Labor Camp

When Jac was arrested, his reaction had been anger, rebellion, fury. Now as he walked toward an empty bunk past dirty sad people—some talking in low voices, some coughing, one throwing up in a slop jar, most silent—he felt disbelief and bewilderment. How had he gotten to this hellish place? What was going to happen to him?

He had arrived just before morning work call. People began to go outside, carrying their bowls and spoons, to line up along a worn path for breakfast. He followed them. He wasn't hungry; he was tired and scared, but he realized he had not eaten since he had left his ship after noon the day before, and he knew he needed food.

Later, he would discover that breakfast at the camp was the first of only two meals a day allowed to prisoners. Outside, each barracks had its own cooking barrel, a steel drum over a small fire. Breakfast and dinner were the same—watered-down potato or cabbage soup and one piece of bread. Jac would learn that a real treat was when a few fish were thrown in the barrel. It wasn't much, just enough to change the taste of the soup a little. Once he got a scale-covered fish head in his soup, complete with eyes and brain. It was a prize full of protein. He ate every bit of it except the scales and teeth. But that was weeks later when he no longer had to fight nausea to keep down the awful daily swill and his diarrhea was under control. Sometimes, as a reward for meeting a work quota, they might be given a real treat—a dish of meal mush, the only grain they received besides the two small pieces of daily bread.

That morning, although he had had no sleep, he was put to work like all the others. He got a glimpse of George and Firsty marching with another group. He tried to smile as he waved at them, wondering if he looked as bewildered as they did. The next day they were able to talk together. They tried to cheer each other up; "Someone will come tomorrow or the next day to straighten this out." "Yeah, damned if we'll give in to these bastards."

"Someone will miss us," Jac insisted. "Maybe that reporter will tell someone—maybe call Murmansk, tell 'em we helped get their new tanker through all that hell. Maybe the captain will send a report to the Allies. They'll know we made it, only to Archangel instead of Murmansk. They'll look for us."

But no one came. Jac kept thinking, Tomorrow, until he lost track of the days.

The sun climbed a little higher and set ever later as the days passed. Darkness of night became dimness of night, but the sky remained drab under high cloud cover. It was cold, but it was a different cold from that aboard ship, drier. At least, Jac thought, I'm not getting a face full of ocean spray every few minutes. He would learn that, when the north wind blew down from the pack ice of the Arctic, the camp became unbearable.

The work camp was engaged in building a railroad—from where to where, Jac never learned. The first week the routine was the same, day after day. He was assigned to a work detail making concrete blocks. At least that's what they were trying to make. The Russians did not seem to know too much about concrete. Traditionally everything in the area had been made from the abundant local timber. But now they had cement, and they were to build equipment and repair shops out of it, buildings large enough to house a railroad locomotive. Over half the blocks they made froze overnight and broke like glass. After a week of failure, they were ordered to move the operation into a wooden work building so that the blocks could be made indoors. Extra stoves were installed. The cement blocks were kept much warmer at night than the workers in their frigid barracks.

George and Firsty were put on a different detail. They were marched out of the camp a half mile or so and put to work driving spikes on a railroad that had almost reached the camp. Other work details were building new barracks. The new buildings had no tenants—yet.

Jac was good at using sign language. He made a few friends among the prisoners, picked up a few words. One or two of them had been professional people and could speak a little English. They knew he was not Russian, but they were not sure they could believe him when he said that he was American. From what he could understand, they were building a new concentration camp for "political prisoners." He wasn't exactly sure what "political prisoners" meant; he had never heard of any at home. The people around him in the camp didn't appear to be criminals—he certainly wasn't one. They weren't enemy soldiers; there were no Germans in the camp. Why would the Russians do this to their own people?

He had not heard much about Russia except in geography class and the glowing propaganda that had been appearing in American news media since Russia had become an Ally. He knew they were Communists, but he hadn't studied much political philosophy. He hadn't learned much from the navy recruits he'd trained at St. Pete. He'd never in his life, as far as he knew, so much as talked to a Communist. So, he hadn't a clue as to why they were all there.

Eventually, Jac learned that many of the people had been in professions—professors, doctors, musicians, writers, artists. These people, who had never needed to do rough work with their hands, now laid rails and cut and hauled timber. Those hands were often cracked, raw, and bloody from the constant friction of frozen hands against frozen tools. It was in the evenings, when their hands were warmed and oozed mucus, that they suffered the most. Jac remembered that his grandfather had once told him a way to keep your hands from becoming sore when hoeing cotton: Urinate on them in the morning; the acid would toughen them. Jac told one of his friends, who passed the advice along. The ones who tried it found that it did seem to help. There was nothing else available.

Trains brought supplies to the end of the line, and prisoners dragged them from there to the camp. There was no mechanized transport. The Soviet Union was at war and could not spare even a single truck for hauling. Carts of various sizes consisted of wooden boxes with wooden axles fitted with solid wooden wheels cut from the trunks of large trees. A long pole served as a wagon tongue, cut to the length needed. This was determined by the number of people the engineers felt would be required to pull whatever load was to be carried in the cart—lumber, cement, cross ties, steel rails, or whatever. The wheels cut from logs never matched. Ice sometimes froze the axles at night in spite of the grease on them. All of that and icy ground added to the agony of pulling them.

Building the road bed for the rails was a task that drove the Russian engineers mad. The ground was frozen solid below the surface. They had no bulldozers, no power shovels, no explosives. Such items went to the war effort. Forced labor was the only available substitute, and Stalin furnished an unending supply.

When it was necessary to cut into a bank or level a small rise in the terrain, picks and shovels, wielded by forced labor, could not do the job. They tried. They spent long days getting nowhere. The engineers were frantic. If they failed to get their railroad built, they might well find themselves prisoners too.

They worked out a solution. Workers were set to cutting and hauling logs to the road bed, where they were laid on top of it and set on fire. This thawed the frozen ground and the underlying permafrost enough that the earth could be shoveled away and the road bed leveled. The rate of progress increased, and because of the fires, the workers were a little warmer than they had been.

Just as the railroad reached the camp, a work party was taken to a spot close to the tracks but some distance from the buildings, and put to work digging a long, deep, open trench. It was very hard work because the ground was frozen.

Then the trains started coming—one, sometimes two a

week. When the first arrived, Jac and one or two others were assigned a new job—ordered to pull small carts to meet the train. When it arrived, the guards motioned for Jac to unlock and open the boxcar door. He knocked the pin loose and slid the door open. What he found was a car packed shoulder to shoulder, nose to chin, with men, some women, and now and then a child or two.

They had been packed in the boxcar for days, getting little food or water. As the door opened and the fresh air reached them, a long low moan rose. They had had no sanitary facilities. Jac stepped back, gagging from the odor, barely restraining the vomit that rose in his throat. Those in the open doorway stood silent, unsure, waiting. A pitiful little girl was moved to the front, holding to her mother's skirt. Suddenly they realized that they were to be allowed to get out of the car, and there was a wild surge for the door.

They stumbled down from the car, all ages, some crying, most silent. Some could not control themselves and had bowel movements on the ground or in their clothes. A body fell out on the ground. No one seemed to pay any attention except to step over it. Many had clothing or a few other possessions tied in a bundle or carried in a small suitcase. When arrested, they were not told where they were going, so much of what they carried were simply beloved personal possessions, quickly gathered—often pitiful little items that were useless in the frozen hell of northern Russia.

After some semblance of order was restored, the people from the cars were given a lecture by "comrade commander," divided into groups, and marched off to the new barracks.

It was then that Jac learned why he had been brought to meet the train. He was ordered to drag out the bodies that remained on the floors of the railroad cars and pile them on his cart. There were always several in each car. Then he was forced to clean up the human filth in the box cars, and when he finished doing that, he and the other members of the work party pulled the carts to the open trench.

The crudely constructed carts, crunching over the frozen ground, bounced and joggled the bodies, causing them to jerk and flop their limbs grotesquely as if in final protest. Many of the dead were older people, some were not. Some were men, some women, one was a little child.

At the trench, Jac had to dump the bodies, spread quick lime over them, and leave them exposed. The open trench would not be covered until it was full. Then another would be dug, and another.

The people who arrived were mostly from Russia, Georgia, the Ukraine; some said they were from Latvia, Estonia, some even from Poland. They were all civilians. Some had been in other camps. They all had been placed on Stalin's "Enemies of the People" list. Many were educated, teachers, professional people, some too important to be left behind in territory now occupied by Germany. Most were kolkhozniks, collective farmers, who had made the mistake of trying to keep enough of what they raised to support their families.

Whatever their political sins, everyone was treated with equality. Each got a spoon, two bowls of soup a day, two slices of bread, one blanket, a bunk thinly padded with lice-infested straw, and unending work.

The Trains

Finally the shock of their internment and the daily life in the camp settled over the Americans. At first they had shown spirit. The guards did not find it amusing to be talked back to, and the Americans were physically beaten to their knees. Reason began to rule. People around them who were beaten, injured, or became sick did not last long under the living conditions at the camp. They determined to stay as fit as they could. They would stay out of the guards' way. They still had a pocketful of rubles. (The soldiers in the truck had taken their watches, but had not searched their pockets.) Money sometimes got them a little extra food. Hardships were easier for Jac to bear—he was young. George and Firsty were well into their thirties, and the life was more difficult for them. When the three could get together, they tried to cheer each other up. Surely someone from the United States would sooner or later take alarm at their disappearance and come searching for them.

When Jac was alone at night, his thoughts were anything but cheerful. Would they, in fact, be missed? They were not on any maritime company's crew list for the convoy. They had sailed with the Russian navy on a ship that had been transferred to Soviet ownership in New York under the Lend-Lease program. They had not been placed on any American personnel or pay records, and the Russians had certainly not turned one in to the Allies. Hundreds of men were reported missing from the convoy. Wouldn't it be assumed that they had simply been lost en route?

None of the other merchant seamen who had arrived safely would know that the three were missing. Even those few friends who had known they were on the Russian ship would figure they had returned home aboard some other ship and then shipped out again. In the Merchant Marine it was not unusual for friends and old shipmates not to see each other for months, even years. Who would think to look for American seamen in a Russian labor camp?

Jac fought against such thoughts. He was afraid of them, afraid of knowing. Knowing that there would be no waking up to rescue, safety, and a free tomorrow.

The trains continued to arrive, one every week or two. The guards looked forward to them. They would meet the trains, even the ones off duty, in order to pick out the most attractive women. Some of the women were single, some married with their husbands, but it didn't matter to the guards. They would come into the barracks at night, as the mood struck them, and summon their choice for a little sexual entertainment. Any who refused took a beating. If the choice was a married woman and her husband tried to prevent them using his wife, he was beaten, often half to death. Some of the guards preferred young men. Whenever the guards appeared, the other prisoners would turn away and look at the wall, to ease the embarrassment and humiliation of the person chosen—and again when they were returned later. It allowed everyone to pretend that no one knew who the pitiful souls were.

In the camp, things of some small value could be bartered with the guards. Money, rings, a young girl's body might be traded for medicine, extra bread, a better job perhaps. They could also be traded to fellow prisoners for an extra bowl of soup, or use of their blanket for a night, and especially for an extra piece of clothing, a pair of gloves, or socks. Jac was very lucky to have had so much clothing on when he was arrested. Especially valuable to his health was his great sheepskin coat and his boots. He also had arrived with a pocketful of rubles. Until it ran out, he used it for extra food for himself and sometimes for those who needed it worse than he did.

The building where he lived was full. The one wood burning stove in the middle of the floor barely kept the frost out. The human smell was awful. The people were not inclined to bathe, especially since there were no facilities. Jac was no different at first, but when he could no longer stand his own smell, he learned one can bathe with snow, at least a little now and then. Washing one's clothes was a little more difficult. You had to take them with you to work while they dried. If you left them behind in the barracks, someone might steal them.

The sanitary facilities consisted of a slit trench outside in the open, just a twelve-inch-wide trench used by both men and women. At night there was one slop bucket inside, sitting in the middle of the floor. It was hard for the women to use it sitting there in the center of the room for all to see. Almost everyone had diarrhea. Sometimes there would be a line of people in the middle of the night pleading for those ahead to hurry. Some lost control and were forced to clean up after themselves. No one looked at them, either out of pity or disgust, or perhaps because they were struggling to control their own heaving stomachs or cramping bowels. Outdoors on work details, some of the women were afraid to pull down their undergarments to relieve themselves in the cold in front of the guards. They preferred to soil their clothing. One could sometimes see the urine on their wool stockings where it froze as it ran down their legs.

If you did not work, you did not eat. Most of the time people who got sick and could not work died, even when friends brought their bowls of soup to them. Some, like a rosy baby-faced young man who bunked near Jac, went mad. He had been the favorite "entertainment" of some of the guards, frequently called upon at night. Now he spent his nights sitting against the wall with his head in his hands mumbling the words, "Jesus Christus, Ave Maria" over and over and over. Those were the only words he spoke at all. He had to be led to work and to get his food. He didn't say his "prayer" during the day in front of the guards or they would beat him. Jac does not know if the boy ever slept. Waking in the night, any night, Jac could hear his liturgy, "Jesus Christus, Ave Maria." Moans and sobs from the darkness of the barracks were the lullabies of the work camp.

The trains were always late. On the days they were to arrive, Jac would be ordered to stand by the tracks and wait. It was always cold. Sometimes he stood waiting in precipitation that was something between wet snow and sleet. He could hear the whistle before he could see the train. At its sound, his mouth would go dry, he would struggle to keep down what little he had in his stomach. Almost hidden by the condensed fog billowing over the hot boiler and hissing steam puffing from the driving pistons, the locomotive jerked and swayed down the uneven tracks toward him, dragging its cargo of wretched souls behind. Brakes locked. Cold steel wheels screeched in protest against cold steel rails, striking sparks of fire. The drab cars, streaked by ice and melting snow, had reached their destination. Once more it was time for Jac to perform his awful task.

After the living were marched away Jac climbed into the filthy rancid cars, grasped the rigid remains of the dead, dragged them to the door, and shoved them out onto the ground. They made a crunching thump against mushy snow or a solid thud where the frozen ground was worn bare. Now and then he found a body stretched out, arms folded, eyes closed as if the person had been made comfortable in his last hours by some caring soul. Most were twisted and warped in the agonizing, grotesque positions they assumed as they collapsed, dying among the feet of those who could still stand. Some lay in their own excrement.

Sometimes there would be a body not quite stiff. These were the worst. The first time Jac reached out and closed his hands around the putty soft flesh of an old man's leg, he did vomit. From then on climbing up into those cars stretched to the limits Jac's ability to control his sanity.

When all the bodies were dumped to the ground and the cars cleaned, Jac would again pull his cart along the train to pick them up for the one last indignity he was forced to commit against them. When the cart reached the common trench grave, he had to throw them in and leave them to stare with hollow eyes until the lime ate them away or a light spring snowfall softly covered them. Jac saw them in his dreams, stiff, twisted, staring at him from their dull dry eyes, their cheeks powdered with lime.

You'll Die Out There

At night a small group would gather around the stove for warmth. There was very little conversation. Jac guessed that it was a feeble attempt at sharing some remnant of human society. In a place where all one's waking hours were expended upon one's own struggle to survive, kindness and comradeship were luxuries no one could afford—except for this brief moment of contact. Sometimes Jac joined them, stealing surreptitious glances at their faces. These held no dignity, no hope, only resignation. It was as if they looked inward, trying to see who they used to be, questioning why such depravity had become their fate.

One night, standing there, Jac suddenly realized that he did not know how long he had stayed in the labor camp. Every day had been exactly the same—dark, cold, dreary, without calendars, without clocks, just one identical exhausting day in an endless trial of survival. As he looked at those around him, he had the chilling feeling that he was looking into his own eyes.

Until then, he had been able to keep his self-image separate from them. He was an American, he was different, a mistake, he shouldn't be here. But now he knew that all of that was gone. I'm one of them! Oh! Dear God! I'll be here forever! Do the mad know they are insane? And if so, does it double the hell they suffer?

The next day after work, he told George that he was leaving.

"How? Where will you go?"

"I don't know,—anywhere but here."

"You'll die out there," George warned him.

"Come with me."

"I'm almost twice your age, I'd never make it. In fact, *you* won't make it. Come on, Jac. Someone will find us. You've got to stay."

Jac replied quietly, "I'll go mad—and then I'll die. I'd rather die out there." He turned and walked slowly toward the gate.

Although the camp was surrounded by barbed wire and guarded by armed soldiers, security was not impossibly tight. After all, the nearest settlement was days away by foot, and without food, equipment, and shelter, no one would stay alive in this Arctic wilderness. If anyone tried it, the guards had only to follow the tracks, and they'd locate the body within a day's walk—if the animals had left anything of it. Why bother to keep a tight guard?

Jac decided to go that night, immediately. It was a dim late afternoon, and he would not be missed until the next morning. The gate was open, left thus for the work parties sent out to cut firewood. Visibility was down to 150 feet, and the swirling wetness would cover his footprints. The guards were more interested in the stoves in the gate houses than in looking out for an escape attempt.

Jac simply walked out of the camp. He had on what was left of the same three pairs of wool pants, shirts, badly worn boots, and sheepskin coat he had been wearing on the night, weeks ago, when he was arrested. He headed toward the point where the sun, last seen, had been setting.

Once he was finally sure that he was not being followed, he became euphoric with the freedom of escape. He walked all that night and the next day. To stop would be to sleep, and to sleep would be to die. In spring the temperature no longer reached minus 40 degrees as was common in midwinter, but it could get cold enough to kill.

He made short rest stops to gather small cones from the pine and fir trees and eat the seeds in them. He had learned this survival trick from his father as a boy in Mississippi. When he had no seeds, he chewed on pine needles. They gave no nourishment as did the seeds, but the bitter sticky taste helped keep him awake. At times he could not avoid the heavy drifts of snow that persisted in shady patches. Walking in two or three feet of wet snow was hard work. Even in the cold one can work up a sweat. From time to time, he would take note of the unique raw beauty of the wilderness: the sun sparkling off the thinning snow, the white trunks of the birch trees against the dark green of the fir and pine. During the short nights, he looked up at the sky and saw the stars. To Jac they appeared to rest on the tree branches. Seen through eyes glazed by the cold, they sparkled with the colored fire of a prism. They danced across the black crystal sky, inviting him west toward the far horizon of freedom. They gave him hope.

Jac had read that careless men, lost in the wilderness, can wander in giant circles, driven by the earth's rotation. He had been taught the stars by fishermen as a child and had learned the skys of oceans that he sailed, studying celestial navigation. Now those same stars would lead him out of the wilderness.

He concentrated on his bearings. He told himself over and over, "Concentrate on nothing else, think of nothing else."

But try as he would, he could not keep his concentration. Hour by hour, the surroundings began to fade away. His fingers began to split from the dry cold. There were numb spots on his face. He could not feel his nose. The rag wrapped around his face was stiff with the frozen condensation of his breath. His lungs burned, his eyes watered. "One foot. Now the other foot. One foot, now the other foot. One foot . . ."

For a while it worried him that he was going to die alone, far from everyone he loved. Then he had a good thought. His body could not sink into the solid ground. He would just fall down and lie there. That would be better than slipping beneath the icy dark ocean like the lost men of convoys. That seemed to make him happy, and he sang for a while, songs from his childhood days at the church camp ground. Long forgotten prayers came back to him. He tried to remember what warm was, tried to remember summers at home, but he couldn't.

"Never mind," he said to himself. "Navigate! You must navigate. How far have I come? Fifty, sixty miles? Let's see. Speed multiplied by time equals distance. How fast? Two miles an hour? Two miles an hour times two and a half days equals . . . equals . . . No, not times days, times hours. O.K.! How many hours in two and a half days? Two and a half times what? Times . . . ?"

He could not quite get it all clear in his mind, could not remember how to solve the problem. In fact, he'd forgotten what the problem had been. It became very hard for Jac to remember anything, to think at all.

But he kept walking. He vaguely knew that he was going to die, but it didn't bother him anymore. Each time he stumbled and fell in the snow, he thought how nice it would be just to lie there for a moment, to rest his aching tired body. But the frozen dead from the trains would come. He could see them standing around him, their joints awkwardly fixed in ridiculous twisted poses. They motioned with curled fingers for him to get up. Some had no eyes, just hollow sockets. They threatened to throw buckets of lime on him. They made him get up, again and again, whenever he fell.

He shuffled now, short stumbling steps, on and on, not quite unconscious, not quite awake. Bells were tinkling somewhere in his brain. Dreamlike bells. He tried to focus his burning eyes. Something was there with him, shapes, moving shapes all around him. Animals, he thought to himself, lots of animals.

One of them spoke to him. It did not seem strange that an animal would speak to him, but he didn't understand the language. He didn't understand where he was. It took all his concentration to focus his eyes. Dimly, he saw big shapes around him, and then a different smaller shape among them. It also spoke to him in a funny language just like the other animals. The figure stepped out from the herd of reindeer.

A rational thought came to Jac: A man, a man with animals. He tried to speak, but he could not quite remember how. The human was short, dressed in colorful felt and fur. He yelled something over his shoulder. Other short people appeared among the reindeer. They spoke to him. He tried to smile, but his lips were terribly cracked. He could not feel his nose. He wondered if he had a nose.

The Reindeer Spoke

The men, all shorter than Jac, gathered around him. Strange, he thought, funny language. His eyes began to focus steadily once again. Slowly he began to think again. With great and agonizing effort, Jac lifted his hands in front of him and crossed his forearms at the wrist, showing by sign that he had been tied, had been a prisoner. Then he pointed toward the east. He then put his shaking hands to his mouth and tried to make eating motions. A man nodded and stepped forward. Jac sank to the ground, darkness closing around him. A second man joined the first and lifted him. Then they carried an American merchant seaman from Biloxi, Mississippi, to a warm tent somewhere in the northwestern wilderness of Russia.

Whether by luck or the hand of Providence, Jac Smith had stumbled into a camp of Laplanders. Friendly but fiercely independent, these people roam an area of some 150,000 square miles as their ancestors have done since time immemorial. The area is called Lapland, even though some of it is located in the Soviet Union, some in Finland, some in Sweden and Norway. To the Lapps, all of it is open; they roam the migration routes of their reindeer herds as they feed on lowland moss and lichens by winter and highland mountain grasses during the short summers. Even the Russians had been unable to persuade them to recognize a border.

The tent, called a *kata*, was cone shaped, stretched over curved poles like the American Plains indian teepee. Inside they laid Jac on skin rugs which covered the floor. On a flat-stone hearth in the center was a small brightly burning cook-fire, its smoke drawn out through a vent at the top of the tent. One of the men held Jac in a sitting position while a woman spooned warm milk from a bowl to his lips. He could not hold a spoon or move his fingers. Several youngsters watched the stranger with curious amusement.

It tasted so good, warm and good. Jac drank all the milk. Then they took his clothes and washed him, applying some sort of salve to his painful face and hands and wrapping him in a fur blanket. They motioned for him to lie down on a bed of leaves and branches near the fire. He had not slept for three days. Now sleep, which a few hours ago would have killed him in the cold, warmly overwhelmed his senses.

He slept for a very long time. When he awoke, he found he had not been left alone. A young man and an older woman were in the tent watching over him. Or were they guarding him? Probably both, he decided. His clothes had been washed and were dry. He smiled at them and fell once again into a warm deep sleep, filled with strange dreams of burning snow and colored stars and dead people and animals that talked.

He opened his eyes suddenly. People in the tent, sitting on the floor, were looking at him. He had screamed, he thought, or was that in his dream? The men had returned. He could smell hot food. He nodded to those around him and said "Thank you." They looked at each other, shaking their heads in agreement that no one understood, but they returned his smile. He then pointed at himself and said, "Jac." Then he did it again. One of the older men pointed at him and said, "Jac!" Jac nodded his head up and down. The group laughed, and two or three said, "Jac!" and so it went around the tent. Jac never could properly pronounce any of their names, but it didn't matter. The spoken word would not be necessary in order for Jac to communicate; his hosts belong to a people who had used sign language in telling stories for centuries.

There was some kind of meat and hot soup for supper. His fingers were still painful, but he managed to hold a bowl in the palm of one hand and a spoon with the other. The simple bowl of soup that night, he was sure, was the most wonderful gift that he would ever receive.

After the meal everyone had something to do. Jac would learn that no waking hour in Lapland was ever wasted. The men oiled and repaired harnesses. One mixed some sort of salve Jac would later see used on the injured hooves of reindeer. One woman was busy cutting skins into patterns. While all this was going on, an occasional visitor from one of the other tents in camp would appear to take a curious look at the stranger they already knew was called Jac. The children, though very cautious and shy, were the most curious. Peeking from behind an adult, their bright dark eyes wide with excitement, they would either duck quickly away or burst into giggles when Jac smiled at them.

A short while later, without any apparent word or signal that Jac could detect, every one put his work away, crawled to his individual mat, and pulled fur blankets over himself. Another day in Lapland had ended.

The morning began with the tinkling sound of the bells on the reindeer. They were hungry and restless and signaled the start of a new day with the sound of a hundred chimes. As each person awoke, he or she rolled up and tied his fur bedding and put it out of the way against the side of the tent even before he got up. While breakfast broth heated, the men pulled on their colorful leggings and felt boots, beautifully made. Soft, beaten sedge or marsh grass filled the boots to act as insulation. It served as a sort of waterproof sock. Supplies of it were prepared every summer and carried with them.

The Lapps broke camp. All the cooking gear, tools, and household goods were packed into a painted wooden chest, a sort of catch-all traveling trunk and the only piece of furniture in the tent. Chairs were not used. Those who were inside would lie on fur rugs padded underneath with leaf and pine branch bedding while they talked, ate, or did their work, and thus they remained below the smoke level.

With no furniture, breaking camp was a simple and practiced art. The tent, skin rugs, and blankets were carefully lashed to saddles placed on pack reindeer, trained for just such work. The chest, tent poles, dried meat, and other food stuffs were placed in sledges pulled by draft reindeer. Some of the sledges, such as those that carried the tent poles, were open; other sledges were closed, to protect their contents from the elements. Some were outfitted to carry one or two people. Jac was put into one of them. The camp was quickly and easily packed, transported, and set up as the herd moved across feeding grounds with the seasons.

While the men and boys tended the herd, the women and small children stayed busy in camp, mending clothes and household wares, making baskets for the coming spring berry season, or weaving and knitting reindeer hair, which was kept in small bundles. They would try to weave an original design each time except for the inclusion of the clan totem, which denoted the maker's family ties. They shaped and polished the small bones of fish, birds, and animals into sewing and knitting needles. Special pouches were made with drawstrings, which they carried for gathering herbs and eatables along the way. Seeing them practice their crafts and skills was fascinating to Jac as he shared daily life with them, slowly regaining his strength. He watched them make all kinds of unguents, powders, and ointments brewed from resins, pine needles, birch and fir-tree bark. Resin was melted into small chewable pieces used to remedy the discomfort of a cough or sore throat. The original cough drop, he thought to himself.

Several girls worked daily on a large reindeer skin. During the time Jac was with them, he watched them begin with a hard dry hide and knead and rub it over and over until it became soft. Then they would take parts of it and continue to work on them until the hide was as pliable and soft as velvet. It took many days and nights of work before a hide was finished. The softest parts were used to make undergarments.

In the evenings while such work was being done, one or two elders would entertain the family by telling stories, or history, or of great deeds, or just plain tall tales, Jac was never quite sure. But he enjoyed them along with every one else because of the wonderful gestures the story teller used. Jac could imagine the strength of the wind by looking at the puffed cheeks, or how deep or tall something was by how many times he raised his hands over his head, or how big or wide by the outstretched arms, or how cold by the way they wrapped their arms around their bodies. Sometimes, Jac decided, the teller's peers, who very likely remembered an event, would judge his truthfulness. One grunt for verification, two for denial. Jac wondered if the story, as he understood it, had anything whatsoever to do with the story everyone else understood. It didn't matter; he thought they were wonderful stories in any event.

Jac noticed that, when they broke camp, putting out the fire was the last act. It was a special ritual, some sort of thanksgiving. Words were spoken while the fire was put out. Jac was never sure just what it all meant, but among these people, whose ancestors had lived for at least two thousand years in this land of ice, he understood that fire was indeed a gift from the gods.

The meals were nourishing—milk, cheese, reindeer meat, dried fish. They sometimes treated him to hot coffee, carefully rationed and much enjoyed. He always wondered how they got coffee.

With good care and good food, Jac regained strength and was soon fit enough to walk with the herdsman when the snow was not too deep. He was not very adept at using snowshoes, but he did learn eventually. In fact, his attempts to master this mode of transportation brought much laughter to the camp. However, the Lapps were very careful to make sure his clothing was adequate, and furnished him with a warm hood and warm mittens.

Brown grasses and some new green shoots began to show in the sunny meadows, but in the shaded forests there was still plenty of snow. They were now passing through terrain that was rising steadily, and in some of the passes through hills, it was especially deep. When Jac got too tired from walking, he was—without asking—placed on one of the sledges. But that happened more and more rarely. Most of the time he walked along with the men, communicating a little by sign language as they attempted to satisfy their curiosity about one another's ways.

The country was starkly beautiful—forest, valleys, frozen lakes, crystal streams running fast and fat with melting snow, meadows, windswept with only sparse dwarf vegetation. When the wind died down, the stillness was intense; the slightest sound carried great distances. It was like no place Jac had ever been. On clear moonless nights you could see by starlight. The air was fresh, rich, heavy in your lungs. Although Jac could rarely see them, there was a surprising variety of animals and birds. He could see tracks in the snow, hear the whirring of wings, glimpse a fleeting white blur. In winter, many northern animals trade in their dark summer colors for white; the arctic fox, owl, hare, and ptarmigan were invisible against the snow. The brown stoat becomes the white ermine. The animals were now slowly turning once again into their darker camouflage of summer.

Jac judged that, by the standards of the Western world, the Lapps would not be considered handsome. They were small in body, had short legs and short skulls, broad faces, concave noses, pointed chins, light skin, and brown eyes. The men had sparse beards and stood between five feet and five feet four. Jac's six feet four inches towered over them. Yet they were very strong physically and personally delightful—friendly, cheerful, curious, with a certain vivacity about them. Jack figured four to six families were traveling together; he could not be sure. Each family seemed to have a minimum of twenty or so reindeer to meet their needs for shelter, clothing, milk, cheese, meat, and tools. Whatever they made, clothes, tools, the smallest of personal items, all were beautifully crafted and heavily decorated. Family members were identified by certain colors and patterns woven into their clothes, boots, and especially their hats. Even tools and utensils made from bone and horn were intricately carved and decorated. Everyone in the family contributed something, even the children. The younger gathered firewood, and learned to do by watching everything the adults did. The older children often left the herd in the early morning and later returned with birds and small animals they had trapped. Jac wondered how they found their way back to the moving herd. The game they bagged added variety to the meals.

They were a self-sufficient people. Sitting in the tent, watching everyone in their colorful clothes busy making things, Jac was reminded of Santa's elves at the North Pole.

His daily life with the Lapps was by no means easy, but after the horror and hardship of the prison camp, he found a certain beauty in the Lappish way of life, their knowledge and skills, their freedom and self-sufficiency. They were a people in harmony with a harsh majestic wilderness.

They moved through forests of stunted pine trees, across vast bogs, copses, and onto the endless white expanse of frozen lakes, now strewn with icy mush. Sometimes the lakes had been swept clear of snow by the spring winds. The ice was carefully tested before the herd was allowed to cross.

Daily the herd spread out, foraging for food, digging down through snow with their sharp hooves to uncover lichens and mosses. Sometimes in the narrow passes, where the snow remained deep, they would dig down until nothing showed but their rumps. If ice was layered too thickly, the Lapps would cut down lichen-covered branches for the animals; they could browse on these until better grazing was reached.

The small bells on the reindeer made them easy to find. The sound was soothing, like the faint tinkle of wind chimes in the distance. Other sounds were equally intriguing: the contented grunting of the herd when on good feed; sometimes the mournful howl of wolves; the occasional bark of an arctic fox; the whirring of birds flying through the heavy, chilled air; the laughter of children.

Standing in the sparkling stillness, Jac could sometimes hear the herdsmen calling to one another far off and the barking of their dogs as they brought strays back to the herd. He was amused by the skill of the dogs. A dog would herd only the deer belonging to its own family, and somehow it knew which animals it was responsible for and paid no attention to the others.

The Lapps knew from Jac's speech cadences that the tall stranger was not Nordic, although he looked it—the flaming red hair of early youth had lightened to strawberry blond. Smith is not sure they ever knew he was American. He had tried all his foreign words on them, a few Swedish and Norwegian learned from shipmates, a few Russian learned at the camp, and lots of Southern American. They just smiled and nodded no matter what he tried. At night he slept in a tent shared by an entire family and their dogs. Always well mannered, he was no threat to them. They accepted him as if finding a lost soul in the wilderness was a normal occurrence—though a new and entertaining event in their lives.

The group moved at the pace of the herd, garnering every morsel of forage. They left the Soviet Union, crossed Finland, climbed the higher elevations of northern Sweden, and finally entered Norway, where the mountains were 3,000 to 4,000 feet high. Jac had no idea where he was, no concept of crossing borders, and only learned the geographical facts much later. He knew the Lapps were generally headed west, and that was enough for him. He also knew that the Russians would put him back in prison, the Swedes, as neutrals, would intern him until the war was over, and the Germans in Finland and occupied Norway would probably shoot him as a spy.

The Lapps well understood that Jac had been in prison somewhere to the east. They must also have known that if they were caught hiding a fugitive, they would be shot, all of them. But they ran the risk without being asked.

There were more and more German patrols around, ski patrols in the highest regions, foot patrols in the snow-free lowlands. Jac could never figure out how the Lapps always knew when one was in the area, but without fail they did. Perhaps, living in the still and barren wilderness, they had much sharper hearing than "civilized" people, undamaged by machines and industrial noise. Perhaps there were always scouts out far ahead and behind acting as lookouts, although Jac never saw them. Whatever it was, they always knew far enough in advance, when the stranger had to be hidden.

They had taught him what to do, although the first time he was a little unsure of their method. They would tie him by his arms and legs tightly under one of the reindeer used as a pack animal. Jac was thin to begin with, and he learned to make himself as small as possible, hanging to the animal's belly. Bundles of skins hung down from both sides of the animal's pack, hiding the fugitive from the German soldiers, who routinely walked through the herds, checked inside tents, searched through sledges, and occasionally invited themselves to a meal. Sometimes they walked along with the group if it was going their way. However long it took, Jac had to remain quietly slung underneath a reindeer, even if his arms and legs grew numb. It was at least warm. Not one of Santa's reindeer could ever be as patient and calm as the animals who kept Jac hidden from the Germans.

He was totally confused about time. He had no idea how long he had been in the Russian labor camp or how long or far he had walked with the Lapps. He knew it was getting warmer, so that it must be nearly summer. The days were longer. Sometimes the herd seemed to move ten, fifteen, twenty miles a day, but he never really knew. The uphill climbing was demanding.

Now that Jac had grown strong and fit, he began to long for home, for meaningful tasks—not just survival—to sail again, to help instead of being helped, to have a hamburger and a shake, to talk to people in his own language. But he trusted his cheerful hosts and kept these yearnings to himself.

Then one day, one of the men motioned for Jac to gather all his possessions, strap on a backpack of food, and follow him. Jac's heart began to beat with the quickening spurs of fear and excitement. Something was about to happen. For good or ill, his sojourn with the Lapps was coming to an end. He struggled to cope with the smiles, the gentle touches, the soft words they gave him, knowing that this was a final farewell. Then he set out with his guide. From a short distance he looked back and waved, and quickly turned to hide his tears, for he knew he would never see his saviors again.

His guide climbed toward the highest ridge of mountains on the western horizon. They walked rapidly for five, maybe six hours, before they stopped in a sparse grove of trees on one side of a small hollow, where the guide motioned for him to stop and sit down. No words passed between them. They waited for what seemed an hour or two. Then from behind a clump of small trees across the hollow, a man stepped out in the open.

He was no Laplander, for he was almost as tall as Jac and much heavier. Has he been there the entire time? Jac wondered.

Jac's friend motioned for him to go to the stranger, who was standing in full view now, some fifty yards distant on the slope across the way. Jac walked slowly, watching the stranger and the area around him. Were there others hidden in the trees?

When he reached the man, he looked back. The Lapp had disappeared. His first reaction was panic. Had he been abandoned? Was this newcomer friend or foe? Could the Lapps have turned him in, perhaps for a reward?

Jac was sure of one thing. He would never return to prison. He turned to run, half-expecting a shot in the back. But then the stranger said one word, which sounded like *Norga.*

Jac whipped around, fighting back tears of relief. He knew that word from crewmen who had sailed with him. The stranger was Norwegian.

In the Hands of Strangers

On April 9, 1940, Germany invaded the neutral countries of Denmark and Norway. The Germans did not want their navy to be bottled up again in the North Sea as in World War I, and occupation of the two Scandinavian countries gave them free access to the Atlantic. Little Denmark could do nothing but submit, but the Norwegians resisted.

Most of the Norwegian merchant fleet, the largest in the North Atlantic, was at sea when the attack came. Hearing the news they reported to England and thereafter made themselves an invaluable part of the Allied supply effort. At home, loyal Norwegians, including remnants of the army which had managed to escape into the mountains, formed Resistance organizations. It was into the hands of the Norwegian Resistance that the Lapps had placed Jac Smith.

Elation filled Jac. This must be Norway! he thought. The Lapps have brought me out of Russia!

Then gradually he sobered down. This new guide was

nothing like the Lapps—cautious and wary of the Germans, but comfortable with each other and the shared danger. This stranger was intense, suspicious, and all business.

All of the Norwegians would be the same. Only later would Smith realize that though he himself was *in* danger, he *was* danger for those who helped him. Their lives depended upon his being what they accepted him to be—an ally, an enemy to Germany. Suppose he turned out to be an imposter, sent to infiltrate their organization and betray them?

Standing there on the slope, the two men eyed each other carefully. They tried to communicate with words. No go. Sign language would have to do. Finally, the newcomer beckoned Jac to follow him.

As he strode along behind his Scandinavian guide, Jac began to sense that there was great danger. This guide, like the Lapps, seemed to have a sixth sense when it came to detecting Germans. It was a good thing—there were lots of them. But here, there were no reindeer to hide under. Were they to be confronted by a patrol, the jig would be up.

In every German-occupied country all citizens were issued identification papers. Anyone caught without papers was immediately taken prisoner and interrogated, no exceptions. Identification papers clearly stated an individual's district and occupation, which, in the case of many of the Resistance guides or couriers, was often listed as woodsman or trapper, occupations that allowed a man to travel in the fields and forest. But no man was allowed outside an area not considered part of his normal daily routine. For this reason Jac would be handed off, one district to another.

Of course, he knew none of this at the time. He didn't even

know the date or where he was or how far he had yet to travel. He had one choice: follow his new guide.

It was daylight. The guide was very cautious, using every terrain feature, every stand of trees to conceal himself and Jac. When they had to move across open ground, they moved fast. Then they would stop, listen, search the surrounding area for any sign of movement. When the guide was satisfied that it was safe, they would move again. Not one word had been spoken between them since they began.

Then Jac slipped and fell into a snow drift and laughed out loud as he had done many times with the Lapps. With lightning speed, the guide clamped his hand over Jac's mouth. Jac looked up at him. The expression on the guide's face made it clear that nothing on this journey would be funny. Jac nodded his understanding, and silently cursed himself for being lax and foolish.

Cold reality replaced his earlier elation: Unlike the Lapps, who were expected to be found in the wilderness and had no reason to conceal their presence, his guide would have no excuse if confronted by the authorities. Jac would not have to be reminded again.

From then on, he moved with deliberate care to make no unnecessary sound, and only hand signals were used between the two men. In the cold still air the sound of a human voice, the breaking of a twig, the falling of a loose rock could carry a great distance. If a curious patrol investigated such sounds, they would very likely find those who made them.

Late in the afternoon they stopped in a small hollow in the shadow of sharply rising terrain. A hundred yards ahead Jac saw a log cabin with smoke rising from its chimney. His guide motioned for him to rest, to make no sound. For over an hour they sat there, the guide watching. Once a man came out of the cabin, looked all around, relieved himself, gathered an armload of firewood and went back inside. Still they waited. At last satisfied, the guide motioned for Jac to follow. They went silently to the cabin, the only sound being the squeaky crunch of their footsteps on the snow that still remained in the shadows.

Inside there were two men, one in his late thirties, one much older. They greeted the guide but did not speak to Jac. The cabin was crude but comfortable, warm. They motioned for Jac to sit by the fire and gave him a plate of smoked fish to eat.

The three Norwegians sat down at a table and talked while they ate. From time to time one or another of them would look or motion toward Smith. At times they argued.

Smith knew they were discussing what to do with him. He had tried to tell his guide that he was American. Unlike the Lapps, Jac thought that perhaps the Norwegian had understood, but from the length of the discussion, he was not sure. He was tall and blond. He could pass for a Dane, or a Norwegian—or a German. Jac will never know what the arguments were about: whether they concerned who he was, who would guide him, where they would take him, or *maybe* whether or not the safest thing to do was to kill him.

Whatever the argument was about, it was finally settled. The older one seemed to be in charge. He motioned for Jac to join them at the table. They shook hands, and Jac was given a silent introduction to the third man, the one who appeared to be in his late thirties. They were not hostile, but they were not overly friendly either. It was strictly business.

The next morning the first guide left. Jac rested all day, sharing meals but no conversation with the two men in the cabin, each of whom took turns standing watch somewhere outside. At dusk the younger of the two motioned for Jac to gather his gear. They were leaving.

The sky was crystal clear. Although there was no moon, the starlight was bright enough so that they could see trees and terrain features. They traveled for the two days following, climbing still higher up difficult terrain still covered with snow. Mountain ranges run north to south the full length of Norway, many exceeding five thousand feet in elevation. They ate dried meat, which Jac found similar to American jerky but with a better taste. It was much colder in the high elevations, but they never made a fire. When they slept, they did so in deep snow that had accumulated under the low branches of fir trees.

His new guide taught him how to dig a small trench, pad the bottom with branches, get in with his sleeping gear, and cover himself with snow. The deeper you dug, the warmer you would be; the wind could not reach you. His guide had a hollow reed that he stuck up through the snow as an air tube, and could cover himself completely. Jac could not bring himself to do that. (Many sailors have a touch of claustrophobia.) He always left a little of his face exposed, protected by the fur of his hood.

At the beginning of each day, the guide checked Jac's condition and then his clothing, especially his foot gear and mittens. He wanted to make sure his charge was not injured by the cold. Success depended on moving fast through harsh country held by the enemy, and a man whose feet suffered frostbite would have to be carried or left behind.

The guide also made sure that Jac's general appearance, seen from a distance, would be accepted as that of a trapper or woodsman. There was still enough snow in the highlands to allow skiing, "corn snow" like that enjoyed in April and May at Colorado resorts. German ski patrols liked to work their way to high terrain, where they had a good field of vision. If, from there, they saw anyone suspicious moving below, they could ski rapidly downhill and check them out. They knew the heights of Norway provided hiding grounds for the Resistance, so Jac and his guide could not afford close inspection.

Late on the second day, they stopped within sight of a tiny shelter cabin, like the warming huts for skiers or climbers that can be found in mountain resorts. Small, maybe eight by six feet, it still offered solid protection from the elements. They watched it for two hours before they approached. Inside, a man was waiting for them. Jac's guide exchanged a greeting that the other seemed to recognize, perhaps some password. They had never asked for Jac's name, never given theirs—in fact, never used names in front of him at all. Thus if they were captured, they could not give each other away.

There was a small store of food in the shelter cabin and a small heating stove with very dry wood that gave off almost no smoke. They ate from the cabin food stash and then replaced it with the fresher food they had brought with them. After a long rest, Jac shook hands with the man who had brought him and left with the new guide, toward freedom.

Smith did not put all of this together at once. At first he felt that he was very close to going home. He had not yet developed sufficient fear of the Germans, and he had absolute confidence in the skills of his guides. They seemed to know everything: the terrain, where shelter could be found, what tree to wait behind for the next contact, where the Germans were. To Jac it became an exciting game, an adventure.

They stayed in the high country, moving very fast. Jac was well conditioned to walking; twenty miles a day was easy enough. But at the pace they were moving over mountainous terrain, he began to wear some. Still, he kept up the pace. Perhaps the sea and a way home were just over the next mountain, or the next.

But there was always another mountain, more Germans. Gradually he began to realize just how perilous his situation was and the threat it posed to those helping him. With each new day, with the sighting of yet another German patrol, with the caution, if not mistrust, shown as he was handed from one group to another, he became more aware of what these intrepid people were risking. If he were caught, not only would he and the guide be shot, but anyone who could be connected with them—the guide's family, maybe a whole village.

Jac often fell asleep trying to understand why so many people dared so much for him. The Lapps were a peaceful people who understood freedom; their kindness was perhaps one more victory in their long saga of survival in the wilderness. But the Norwegians were different. It had to be more than kindness to a stranger in difficult circumstances.

Were they simply interested in helping any enemy of the Germans? Or was his deliverance their small victory over an all-powerful enemy? Or was it a simple act of mercy?

Whatever the case, Jac was profoundly grateful to them. He made up his mind that he would respond quickly and exactly to every direction given him. He would make no mistakes. He would question nothing.

The Sea!

Long after he had lost count of the endless changes of guides, each handoff a repetition of the one before, Jac was brought to his first family setting in Norway. He and the guide were moving southwesterly now on slopes that descended through heavy forests. He followed his guide into a clearing, and there it was, a real home with out buildings and farm animals. It was built of heavy timbers, similar to the pioneer cabins of the American frontier. A man came out to greet them, speaking loud and clear and making no attempt to conceal their arrival. He apparently recognized Jac's guide and welcomed him warmly. He nodded genially at Jac and invited the two into the house.

The house was laid out so that the adults slept in a room which was partitioned off from the rest of the cabin, which was a combination kitchen and living area with a large fireplace. Over the adults' bedroom there was a loft, where the children slept. Jac was impressed by their abundance of warm clothing and covers made from furs. The furniture was beautifully and sturdily built, the seats of the chairs covered with skins. Everything seemed to be hand made. The house itself, as well as small items, was decorated with carvings of animals and birds, sometimes employing real animal horns, claws, or teeth.

A woman worked at the stove. A small boy and a little blond girl stared at him from their perch in the loft. Shortly the woman brought over two hot bowls of broth and fresh bread. It was the first hot food Jac had tasted in a long time. The cabin owner and the guide talked for a while, and then the guide rose and put on his coat and pack, now full of fresh food. He shook Jac's hand and gave a bear hug to the owner. Jac walked out with him and watched as he climbed the hill in the direction from which they had come.

Jac sensed a feeling of safety around him. The family was friendly, there was no detectable presence of fear. The children laughed and romped. That evening they had a fine supper of wild game and potatoes. Then a soft pallet with warm blankets was laid for Jac in front of the fireplace. Completely exhausted, he fell asleep, too tired to dream of Germans or the dead from the trains or floating bodies in the sea. The next day, the little girl took a wooden bucket with a leather strap on it and went out to the small stable to milk the cow. When she brought the fresh milk into the house, her mother made thick cakes, like pancakes only much thicker. They were hearty and delicious.

Later in the morning a young man came for Jac. To Jac he seemed hardly more than a boy, but when they compared ages in sign language it turned out that he was about Jac's age. But Jac had by then forgotten that he was a young man himself. He felt old and worn.

His new guide was a husky handsome fellow with brilliant blue eyes, light blond hair, and cheeks like polished apples. All the other guides had appeared at least twice this boy's age. Did he know what he was doing?

They walked all day and into the night, skirting downwind of the scattered farms that began to appear, so their dogs would not bark. They never used roads. The weather was getting better, warmer during daylight. Just before dawn they stopped in a grove of fir trees, where they rested and ate a snack. This was the first person that Jac had run across who could speak a few words of English. "Come," "yes," and "no" was about all he could manage, but it was wonderful to hear nonetheless.

The boy told Jac to stay where he was and left for a long time. Jac slept. It was nearly noon before the guide returned and motioned for Smith to follow him. They came over a ridge and could see a small trading settlement in the valley below, just a handful of houses and outbuildings. It was the site of a monthly market or trading day for people who lived in the surrounding area. They walked down to the settlement, trying to appear calm and natural, and arrived at the back door of one of the houses. There the boy knocked on the door—not a normal knock, but some sort of signal. The door cracked open, and someone inside looked them over for a moment or two, exchanged a few words with the boy, and then let them into the building. Jac went immediately to the fire to warm himself. After a hot lunch was served from the stove by an older woman, Jac was shown upstairs to a bed, the first real bed he had been offered since he left his ship, which seemed a hundred years ago.

He undressed for the first time since he had left the Lapps. There was a pitcher of water and a bowl on the dressing table with real soap and a towel. The water was cold, but he didn't mind. Feeling clean and fresh he pulled back the sheets and slipped into the wonderful comfort of a feather bed. He didn't want to fall asleep right away—not before he had savored the luxury of lying between clean sheets in a real bed—but sleep fell heavily upon him. He slept all the rest of the day. At midnight he was awakened by his young guide. The only light was the light of the fire, for none of the oil lamps were lighted. "Come," the boy said and handed him his clothes. They smelled fresh and clean. Jac got dressed, thanked his host, and once more followed his guide into the darkness.

By late afternoon of the second day, they came upon an older man standing at the edge of a field with a wooden walking staff in his hand. The boy walked straight up to him with Smith just behind. The two spoke briefly. Jac could only make out a hearty "Yah! Yah!" from the older man. Then the boy turned, put his hand on Jac's shoulder, smiled, and walked away. The old man picked up a rucksack, motioned for Jac to follow, and took off at a surprising clip. They were moving south southwest and down from the higher country. They walked all day and most of the night, never resting for more than ten minutes at a time. Jac, breathing hard and bone tired, thought to himself, The older the guides get, the harder it is to keep up with them.

The terrain began to change. Although the valley walls were steep, the forest grew thicker on their sides while the valley floor was more open. They saw more farms and more people. There were fewer places to use as cover. Jac became tense. His guide indicated he had to be nonchalant, to simply walk past anyone that happened along. He had to remind Jac, who was very apprehensive, to stop looking all around. Jac realized the man was right. The natives didn't need to look around; they had seen the area before and weren't concerned if anyone saw them. Any action on Smith's part that looked the least suspicious could be fatal. In addition to the Germans, there were always traitors present, ready to reap a reward from their German masters in exchange for useful information. It was very hard for Jac to saunter casually down the road, looking as though he hadn't a care in the world, but there were times when the guides could not avoid using certain roads or bridges. Melting snow had turned creeks and streams into raging rivers impossible to wade. He had to master an air of confident ordinariness.

There were several "safe" houses where he was given shelter in areas considered too dangerous for travel by day. New guides would come for him when it was safe to move again. He was sometimes transported by truck or wagon, which greatly increased the distance covered in a day, but he was always guided on foot across district borders or other known checkpoints where vehicles were routinely searched.

In several of the houses, he witnessed activities that told him his hosts were doing more than smuggle strangers. In one house, two women, one middle-aged, the other in her early twenties, spent hours loading ammunition into clips and cleaning pistols, rifles, and one or two automatic weapons. In another, he and his guide waited until a young girl returned from a trip into the village to get the latest information on German and police activity in the area. Women were often more effective as couriers than men. It was normal for them to be in a village market or to travel to another village to see a relative. Since there was a shortage of doctors, midwifery was a common practice, and midwives were allowed to travel over a wide area in the normal performance of their medical practice. So midwives became important couriers. Only top leaders and couriers knew how to contact other Resistance cells directly. In this way if one cell fell, it could not compromise another.

Jac learned all this from what he saw and inferred. He was never told anything unnecessarily. Thus, if captured and tortured, he could reveal no real names, nor could he retrace his escape route. He didn't even know how his guides found their way over such distances in rough terrain in the dark. Most of the time he had no idea where he was, but he reasoned that he must be getting nearer to the coast: The carvings decorating the homes had changed from motifs depicting animals, birds, and forests to those showing carved fish, anchors, rope borders, and boats.

On one memorable day, an older guide came for Jac— older but very fit. He set a hard pace as the ground grew rocky. Jac could barely keep up with him.

And then Jac sensed something in the air that put wings on his feet. He smelled it before he could see it. *The ocean!* That salty tang—they had to be getting close to the sea.

He began to feel dampness on his cheeks; then he could see mist blowing up the valley they were descending. Finally he realized it wasn't a valley—it was a fiord.

By midmorning he could see in the distance a body of water with a rocky coastline. He felt elated. Soon, below him, he could clearly make out the water as they moved toward the mouth of the fiord. By late afternoon they came upon a fishing village on one side of a small natural harbor. Jac counted fifteen fishing smacks, some with nets hanging in the water, others with them piled on deck. They were not unlike the Biloxi trawlers, only larger with more draft and greater freeboard, and constructed, he reasoned, a little more stoutly for the demanding conditions of the Norwegian Sea.

The fishing boats put the final touch to his excitement. He was thrilled beyond speech. He had reached the ocean! It was a sight he had sometimes thought he would never see again.

They approached the harbor from the far side and waited. Presently a man came along, who stopped and talked a long time with the guide. They seemed to pay no attention to Jac. Then the man left, and once again they started off down the coastline. They walked all the rest of the day until early evening.

Finally they stopped, and Jac was told to wait among the rocks above the beach. His guide left and did not return until after midnight. He motioned for Jac to follow him around a little point of land. Jac's heart leaped to his throat. There, just beyond the shoreline, he could make out the dark silhouette of a fishing trawler, its engine idling quietly, showing no lights. His guide motioned toward the boat and nodded good-bye. The boat eased in a few yards on the calm water until the bow touched a large rock. Jac was pulled on board by the boat's lone master.

They entered the pilot house and the captain eased the craft out into the dim, mist-shrouded inlet. The skipper tried to communicate using a sort of Norse-English. For the first time, Jac felt that someone understood, really believed that he was American. There had not been much American activity in that part of the world, except for a few seaman who had washed ashore as survivors from the Murmansk run. His guides had probably recognized his speech as a form of English, but because he had arrived from the east, it is doubtful that they realized he was an American. But this skipper seemed to understand, perhaps because he listened to BBC broadcast in English or had visited British ports. In fact, many Norwegians had emigrated to the United States. Who knows? thought Jac. Maybe he has a cousin in Minnesota.

The captain fixed Jac a steaming cup of tea with lots of sugar. It was the first sugar he had tasted since he left the *Cedar Creek.* It was wonderful! The old skipper was wonderful! Feeling a deck beneath his feet and the roll of the sea was wonderful. He was home.

A short time later, they reached the island of Florö a few miles off the mainland. There the captain slipped in quietly and docked among the other boats in a small harbor.

The captain showed him to a bunk and gave him a couple of old blankets. He told Jac not to go up on deck, not to move around, to make no noise, to speak to no one, to answer no call from the dock. Then he left.

Smith welcomed a chance to rest and slept for what seemed a long time. When he awoke, he heard the captain and another man in a serious discussion. They both smoked pipes as they talked, and occasionally looked over at Jac. Then, apparently, everything was settled. Jac went back to sleep and did not awaken until he heard the sound of engines starting.

All the boats on the island moved out of the little harbor together, their bows slicing into the seas, headed as usual for their fishing grounds. But Jac sensed that the atmosphere was tense.

There was good reason for tension. He did not know it, but he had taken what the British Commando Headquarters and the British intelligence community referred to as the Shetland Bus.

The Shetland Bus

The Export Group of the Norwegian Resistance ran this hazardous service. Using the cover of Norway's fishing fleets, composed of small trawlers and smacks, the Export Group made clandestine runs between Norway and the Shetland Islands or mainland Scotland. During the course of the war, over countless trips, the Shetland Bus delivered more than four hundred tons of arms, ammunition, and explosives to Norway, as well as free Norwegian forces and British secret agents. In return they delivered refugees, rescued Allied seamen, and resistance members who were known to be in danger of arrest. Over three hundred such souls were ferried to Scotland. O. M. Smith, Jr., would be another one of them—if they made it.

It has been said that never in history have so many small boats and their crews been deliberately and repeatedly risked in such stormy and treacherous seas. Some boats were lost, but the price on shore could be even higher.

One cell of the Export Group was successfully infiltrated

by the Nazis. A member of the group was picked up and questioned by the Gestapo. They burned the palms of his hands with a soldering iron and then told him, since he had experienced the pain on a less sensitive part of his body, wouldn't he rather talk than feel the iron on his really tender parts? After he did feel the pain, after they removed a few fingernails, after they had broken all the fingers on his right hand, a fishing boat carrying two British agents was intercepted at the coastal village of Televaag.

Trapped at the dock, the agents opened fire with automatic weapons. One of them was killed, the other wounded and taken alive. He was the more unlucky of the two. A German officer and several of his troops had been killed. In retaliation, all of the men in the village, sixteen years old and above, were interred in labor camps, where most were worked to death. All of the fishing boats were sunk. All the houses, three hundred of them, were burned.

Until well offshore, the fishing boats remained in contact. Gradually, while fishing, they spread farther and farther apart. Jac's boat never altered course. The vessel would pause now and then, and the two of them would put over a net to give the appearance of fishing, since the Germans monitored the fishing fleet with patrol planes. When the captain reached a point considered beyond the limits of the patrol planes, he dropped all pretense and ran for it.

The next morning when Jac awoke, he could not see a single boat. They were moving on a steady course and not sparing the engine. He did not have much to do until the captain pointed out a stray mine in the distance bobbing in the sea. Jac understood, and spent much of his time as lookout for mines—German mines, British mines, mines dropped from planes, mines which had broken their tethers, and were drifting, uncharted and a menace to friend and foe alike.

The next morning the wind was relatively light, but they were sailing in a mist-shrouded ocean of huge uncomfortable swells rolling relentlessly onward. Though the swells were steep, they were not breaking. The bow of the heavy trawler would sink into the oncoming hill of dark water, almost dipping into it before it slowly rose to its peak. Then the bow would hang momentarily at the crest before plunging down again, the stern lifting and falling in its turn as the wave moved from under them. Jac, his coat pulled tightly around him, stood outside, forward of the pilot house, watching the sea. He had known fear many times, but what appeared before him now raised the hair on the back of his neck as nothing had before. Through the mist just ahead the water moved in a strange surging pattern. Slowly a great monster boiled up to the surface, streaming tendrils of seaweed from its steel spines, which seemed to stare through the green slime like hundreds of eyes.

Jac screamed out to the captain, motioning frantically for him to alter course. Then, with gurgling and sucking sounds, the mine was swallowed into the sea again—directly in front of the bow. Jac could not breathe as he felt the vessel veer slowly away from the monster's path. And then the mine surfaced again, swirling water pouring off its spherical bulk as it rose beside the trawler, its fragile detonator spines within inches of the hull. Jac watched motionless, mesmerized, as the rolling monster slid past and disappeared into the frothy spume of the trawler's wake. Only then did he breathe again.

When a landfall was finally made, Jac was thrilled but confused. The captain appeared to turn away and go offshore again. Jac knew the skipper was navigating by dead reckoning, so he assumed that he had checked his position by known landmarks and was now headed for the place he intended to dock.

The Shetland Bus skippers navigated by compass, time, and distance, plus experienced guesses as to the effects of tide and weather. The fishing fleet was allowed no ocean charts, no maps of Scotland, no sextants or other equipment. If a fishing captain was caught by the Germans in possession of such things, he was immediately arrested. But dead reckoning had permitted their Viking ancestors to cross these same waters in open boats, and Jac's skipper was making it work for him now.

(We do not know for certain, but it is likely that the first landfall Jac saw was the Shetland Islands and that the captain then turned for a direct course past Fair Island and the Orkneys to a point of land off Aberdeenshire called Rattray Head and thence south a few miles to the port of Aberdeen.)

One morning at daybreak the port of Aberdeen appeared dead ahead. It was easy to see the captain had been there before. He took out a flash light, signaled the harbor, and received an immediate recognition signal in return. The submarine nets were opened just enough to allow the small craft to enter. A motor launch intercepted them and signaled, "Follow me." They were directed to a dock where several other similar small vessels were tied up. Two naval officers boarded, along with the usual representative from the harbormaster's office. One of the naval officers greeted the captain with obvious familiarity, and then asked Jac to sit down for a chat. The captain nodded to Smith, and walked off down the pier with the harbor official.

Just What Were You Doing in Norway?

The senior officer offered Jac a cigarette, lighted up one himself, and while the junior officer got out pen and paper, said, "Suppose you just tell us what you were doing in Norway."

Two and a half hours later the junior officer put away his notes. "Quite a lucky fellow, I'd say." The senior officer added, "A most interesting story, Boatswain Smith, most interesting indeed."

The British naval officers simply did not believe Jac's story. They did not say so outright, but with cool reserve they told him, "We're afraid you'll have to come with us to the Admiralty. Routine in a case like yours, you know. They'll have a few more questions to ask."

O. M. Smith crowded into a small Austin sedan with the officers and their driver, who was a young Wren (Women's Royal Naval Service) in naval uniform. Her presence made him acutely aware of his shabby clothes and ashamed of the fact that he had not had a real bath in a long time. She drove them to the Admiralty. It was a typical wartime compound, administration buildings, naval barracks, dining hall, all fenced in and patrolled by guards. Smith was ushered into a utilitarian hall, offered another cigarette and a chair, and told to wait there while the two Royal Navy lieutenants went into an office marked "Intelligence."

About thirty minutes later Jac was shown into the office, where he was asked to tell his story to the officer in charge. The commander could not believe such an incredible story either. After hot tea was served, he told Jac, "I frankly don't know what to make of you, Boatswain Smith. Here you show up with no papers and the most fantastic story we have ever heard from a seaman. We are checking with the Yank authorities but so far have turned up nothing. I'm afraid you'll have to go before a board of inquiry. Hope you understand."

Jac understood. They thought he might be a spy. He just didn't know what he could do about it.

British Naval Intelligence had run into English-speaking German infiltrators before, most with stories that became untraceable at some point. Often they assumed the identity of a dead person, whose story they knew would check out. If this fellow with his fantastic story was one of them, he could compromise at least one cell of the Shetland Bus, and maybe several cells of the Resistance.

He was assigned a room and allowed to move about within the compound, but he could not leave. A couple of British sailors were assigned to "escort" him. He was taken to another building and shown to a small room and handed a shaving kit and a towel. Down the hall he found a shower. He washed himself and his clothes and dried them on a radiator. Shabby and clean was better than shabby and smelly. He and his shadows had supper in the dining hall that night.

Afterward they offered him English cigarettes, a brand labeled Passing Clouds, which had sort of a built-in cigarette holder—not a filter, but a hollow paper mouthpiece. Jac took one, shared a light with one of his escorts, and watched as the mess hall was turned into a movie theater. A screen and projector were set up in the dining hall, and officers and men alike came in to watch a new Greer Garson film. The food had been filling, the movie a renewed taste of a familiar culture, but his full enjoyment of them was limited by the fact that he was still not free, and the nagging thought that, after all he had been through, he might still be detained as a spy— or even hung. He had told his life story, the absolute truth of everything he knew, but no one seemed able to locate any official records to back up his claim that he had sailed with the Russians to Archangel.

The next morning Jac was ushered into a conference room for the board of inquiry. He was seated in a chair facing eight or so officers with a British naval captain presiding.

They seemed interested, even fascinated, as Boatswain Smith once again told his entire story. There were two Wrens present, kept busy running in and out of the room, taking messages handed to them by the various board members, and returning messages to them. Jac assumed they were getting verification for some of the answers and facts he gave them. At one point the presiding captain said, "Mr. Smith, you say you are from Biloxi, Mississippi. Have you heard of Pascagoula?"

"Yes, sir."

"Where is it?"

"On the coast of Mississippi about eighteen miles east of Biloxi."

"Do you know the name of a shipyard there?"

"Yes, sir, it's Ingalls," replied Jac.

It turned out that the officer had been there to examine one of the ships Ingalls had built for the Royal Navy.

At ten o'clock sharp, they all took a break while tea was served. Then there were more questions, and then lunch. Finally late in the afternoon, the presiding captain asked, "Well, Mr. Smith, just what is it you want?"

Jac's answer was simple: "I want to go home."

The next morning, Jac was escorted to the Admiralty Office in Glasgow. He believes it was on Sauchiehall Street. From Glasgow he was sent to the Admiralty Offices in Liverpool, housed in an old Victorian building on High Street near the Mersey River.

There he was sent in to a commander's office. The officer looked up, closing a folder on his desk. Jac, standing across the desk, saw his name and the word "secret" stamped on the cover.

"Mr. Smith," the commander said, "I know you don't have any money and only the clothes on your back. We can't do much about that, I'm afraid, your being a merchant seaman and not a member of any armed service. However, here is a railroad pass, meal tickets, and a railroad schedule with your route marked on the back. It will get you to Milford Haven, Wales, where we've arranged for you to be taken aboard an American ship in a convoy bound for New York tonight. It's the best we can do. You'll have to leave straight away—you barely have time to make it."

The officer handed Jac the packet containing his tickets and said, "There is one other thing: We ask that you not discuss your story with anyone, especially how you got to Scotland. If such information fell into the wrong hands, it could place the people who helped you in a bad spot. You do understand, don't you?"

Jac nodded vigorously. He understood only too well.

"Fine then." The commander stood up. "Remarkable story, really." He walked around the desk and shook Jac's hand. "Well, good sailing, Mr. Smith."

Jac was driven to the railroad station in Liverpool, where he caught the train to London. He changed trains at Paddington Station, and he was to transfer again at Bristol for Milford Haven. Exhausted, he asked a lady in his compartment to please wake him at Bristol should he fall asleep.

"Better wake up, young fellow." It was the conductor. The lady who had said she would wake him at Bristol was gone. When Jac asked where he was, he was shocked to find out that he was at Pengathen, well down the Cornwall peninsula past Bristol. It was dark out. The conductor, when told of the situation, got Jac on another train back to Bristol. At a dead run, he made the last train from Bristol to Milford Haven.

"You're cutting it a bit close, aren't you, Yank?" said a perky young Wren at the harbor office in old Fort Hubbelston. It was almost eleven at night. "Another five minutes, and you would have missed the convoy. Come along now, you just might make it."

Jac followed the young woman down to the dock where a tug was waiting, engine running. He followed the Wren on board. She turned and said, "How about throwing the lines off for me," and climbed into the empty pilot house. Jac was surprised that she skippered the tug, and did it alone.

She skillfully maneuvered the tug out into a harbor that

was pitch black. Not a light. Jac could barely make out the dark shapes of ships at anchor as the tug threaded its way among them. The entire time since his arrival in Britain he had noticed an unusually large number of both British and American soldiers and sailors everywhere—trains crowded with them, roads filled with truckloads of them. Now, as his eyes became accustomed to the darkness of the harbor black-out, he realized he had never seen so many ships of all types crowded into an anchorage. Many of them were riding high, emptied of their cargo. Others lay waiting to be unloaded. Something special must be going on, he thought.

Jac was impressed with the skill of the young Wren, pushing the tug across the harbor. He could never have found a specific ship anchored among all the black shapes crowding the darkness. Yet she took him directly to the ship that was expecting him. As chance would have it, it was a T-2 tanker. He truly had barely made it. The deck crew was weighing anchor as the tug came alongside. Jac thanked the lady and scrambled up the ladder that had been put over the side for him.

Home

It was September 1, 1944. The tanker was the *White Horse*, identical in every way to the *Cedar Creek*. Her captain was a Norwegian named Trygve Wold. Although a passenger, Jac felt at home. Members of the crew, true to the custom of respecting the personal life of fellow crewmen, did not pry into the circumstances that had led Jac aboard their ship in the middle of the night with nothing but the clothes on his back. They accepted him as a fellow seaman, and from among them he gratefully accepted a clean change of clothing, almost his size. He had the good feeling that he belonged there.

The convoy swiftly formed and headed west. Jac learned why so many ships had been at Milford Haven. They were supplying support to the Allied army now fighting in western Europe. The greatest amphibious assault the world had ever seen, D-Day, had taken place almost three months before on the sixth of June. The summer of 1944 was gone. Jac was amazed by the passage of time, by all that had happened in the world since last April. But he was most exhilarated to be aboard a ship again, a ship headed home.

Both the Germans and the North Atlantic were reasonable to the convoy as it steamed westward. However, there was one more trial in store for Jac and the *White Horse* before they reached the United States.

A few hundred miles from New York the radio operator handed a weather report to Captain Wold: "12 Sept.44. 0700 hrs. Hurricane due east of Miami. Winds, 140 miles per hour. Storm moving north northeast."

That storm was eventually christened by the U.S. Weather Bureau the Great Atlantic Hurricane. A new storm-tracking system had been introduced. The storm's position was being reported by naval reconnaissance planes. At the time, few planes had ever been deliberately flown into a hurricane. One pilot reported the weather so violent that "it took all the strength of myself and the co-pilot to control the plane." Back at its base, it was found that over two hundred rivets had been sheared off each wing.

Two days later the *White Horse* received a second message: "Sept. 14, 1944, 7:00 AM. Hurricane centered east of Cape Hatteras. Winds 145 miles per hour, gusts stronger. Moving north northeast. Expected to go ashore vicinity New York."

The hurricane had boiled up out of the Caribbean and Gulf of Mexico and was headed straight for New York. The *White Horse* was in between. Her captain considered it only a minor inconvenience.

Captain Wold was very short, especially for a Norwegian. He had a box made from mahogany upon which he stood for better visibility from the wheelhouse. On this dark night he was having a bit of trouble keeping his box from moving about. To her crew, the *White Horse* looked more like a submarine running on the surface than a tanker. They were in the middle of the hurricane, 140-mile-an-hour winds, fifty-maybe sixty-foot seas. The bow lookouts had long since been called in; no one could survive on the forward deck, and if something got in front of the ship, damn little could be done about it anyway.

The captain, first officer, helmsman, a steward trying to hold on to a pot of coffee, and Jac were all in the wheelhouse clinging to the storm rails or anything else they could hold on to. The steward, gray as a ghost, asked, "Captain, are you scared?" Captain Wold stood a little taller on his box, and without taking his eyes off the bow, which at the time had disappeared beneath a huge sea, replied, "Nothing to be scared about. *White Horse* is good ship. Maybe bang up deck gear a little. She will ride it out like the horse she is."

He turned toward the men and allowed himself a slight smile. Captain Wold first went to sea on a sailing vessel at the age of sixteen. In the sixty-eighth year of his life, he was riding out the fifteenth hurricane he had encountered at sea.

When the storm had passed, it was discovered that, as Captain Wold had predicted, *White Horse* had one smashed lifeboat, one missing, completely torn away from its davits, and various other damaged and missing pieces of deck gear. Her position was 129 miles farther away from New York than she had been when the storm overtook her. But she had endured. . . .

And, so had O. M. (Jac) Smith, Jr. He was twenty years old.

Once ashore, in borrowed clothes, Jac called on the Coast Guard, the Maritime Administration, the Seaman's Union Hall, and his old employer, Maritime Transport Line. They all listened, they all were sympathetic, some even believed him.

None could find any records that would back up his claim that any of them owed him American dollars for his convoy duty on a Russian ship (nor did he ever receive any).

He reported to all the above, as he had to the British, that two of his shipmates were being held in a Russian labor camp somewhere out of Archangel. (After the war, at an emotional reunion, he and George Borrkle got together. Jac discovered that George had been released in 1945 just before war's end. Neither he nor George ever knew what happened to the engineer they called Firsty.)

Marine Transport Line, based on his previous company record and the recommendation of Captain Wold, offered Jac the position of boatswain aboard the *White Horse.* Captain Wold had been impressed with Jac and his knowledge of a T-2 tanker. Jac thought about it. A lot of people had risked a great deal to get him back to his job, transporting the material that would win the war. He was a tankerman, it was his trade.

He called home. It was at first an emotional event. Mrs. Smith thanked God her son was safe. Then, like all mothers, she indicated that maybe he wasn't as good a son as she had raised him to be. The idea of not writing all that time! Worrying his family half to death! They had been unable to find anyone who knew where he was or what he was doing. Where had he been anyway?

Jac thought about it a moment. He had been asked to say nothing about how he had gotten out of Russia, nothing that would endanger those who had helped him. He told his mother that he had been on a secret convoy, which was really the truth. Then he said there was a war on, he was going to sea again. "Love you, Mom, tell everyone hello for me."

Epilogue

Jac went back to sea, back to the convoys and the cold. Eventually the *White Horse* was ordered to the Pacific, and he served many months carrying fuel to fighting units all over that ocean. Japanese submarines had been pretty much wiped out by then, but the *White Horse* had her share of kamikazes to fight off at the invasion of Okinawa. A few months later the war was over.

When Jac and his fellow merchant seamen returned home, there were no parades for them, no G.I. Bill for college educations, no veterans' hospitals for the broken ones. They simply came home from work.

After the war, Jac returned to the sea and sailed to "all of the islands under the horizon." Once, by chance, in a bar in Brazil, a remarkable coincidence occurred. Jac was having a beer with a new young crew member named Cori Linguis, whose brother, he discovered, had been the light-heavyweight champion boxer of Norway. Jac told him of his escape from Russia and the aid given him by the Norwegian Resistance. Linguis stopped him suddenly and said, "You're the one—the American my grandmother told me about. Her name was Sorenson, and you stayed one night in her house." And then he described a house and a village just as Jac remembered them.

So they *had* known he was an American.

Jac sailed into two more combat zones, Korea and Vietnam, before he came ashore for good. Although he passed the examinations to qualify for a master's license, he was rejected when he tested color blind during the physical. So he continued sailing—except for one year. It was near the end of his career when Jac decided it was time to find some small way of returning the generosity and helpfulness shown to him by caring strangers around the world. He became a caring stranger himself by teaching English to children at the Muslim Academy of Indonesia on the island of Sulawesi, Indonesia. It was one of the most enjoyable years of his life. He left to return home only after receiving word that his father had a fatal illness.

He came home to Biloxi. Home, to live a quiet life looking after his elderly mother and a golden retriever named Julius Caesar. (His mother never knew what her son had been through until she read the draft of this book. She told the author quietly, "I thought it must have been something like that. He never talked about it. Never would tell me.")

On January 19, 1988, more than forty-two years after the end of World War II, the U.S. Government finally granted veteran's status to "any civilian sailor who served on an ocean-going merchant ship during the period of armed conflict in World War II."

Of some 250,000 who served, it is estimated that perhaps

50,000 or so are still living. Many who needed help wound up ashore on Skid Row, forgotten in some flophouse, fighting their own private ghosts. Even during the war, studies were made which showed that "convoy fatigue" was taking its toll on merchant seamen. One such study said, "Countless nerve-torn men would survive another voyage only to come ashore, lock themselves in a lonely hotel room, and try to drink down the horrible memories until time to ship out again."

In January 1943 another study reported, "They go to sea, and back to sea, and back to sea again, until one wonders how it is possible to face the continued expectation of death or long chances against survival. Those who have suffered the most seem the most anxious to get back to sea."

The ships were always manned.

On October 2, 1988, O. M. Smith, Jr., received an envelope from the government. In it was a certificate of Honorable Discharge, making him eligible for some veterans' benefits. When he showed it to the author, who was researching this story at the time, he said sadly, "It really doesn't matter anymore. It is too late for most of my shipmates, except maybe for a few tombstones and flags."

Jac is not a sad or bitter man. He loves music, knows history, art, most subjects one might mention. He has retired from his job as a bridgetender. He lives in the present with awareness, and unselfishly participates in the civic and social activities of his city. He goes fishing when the mood strikes him.

Although he will deny it, he is an example of many quiet American heroes, who ask for nothing, but who deserve at least a salute in passing—if only for the wake of freedom they leave behind.

Bibliography

Bang, Per. *Norway.* Hamlyn, 1971.

Bekker, Cajus. *Hitler's Naval War.* Translated by Frank Ziegler. Garden City: Doubleday & Company, 1974.

British People at War. Long Acre, London: Odhams Press, Ltd., 1943.

Buchheim, Lothar-Gunther. *U-Boat War.* Translated by Gudie Lawaetz. New York: Alfred A Knopf, 1978.

Bunker, John Gorley. *Liberty Ships.* Annapolis: Naval Institute Press, 1972.

Carse, Robert. *Lifeline.* New York: William Morrow & Co., 1944.

Collinder, Bjorn. *The Lapps.* Princeton, N.J.: Princeton University Press, 1949.

Creswell, John. *Sea Warfare 1939–1945.* Berkeley: University of California Press, 1967.

Gibson, Charles Dana. *Ordeal of Convoy N.Y. 119.* New York: South Street Seaport Museum, 1973.

Hautzig, Esther. *The Endless Steppe: Growing Up in Siberia.* New York: T. Y. Crowell Co., 1968.

Hughes, Terry, and John Costello. *The Battle of the Atlantic.* New York: Dial Press, 1977.

Hurd, Sir Archibald, ed. *Britain's Merchant Navy.* Long Acre, London: Odhams Press, Ltd., 1943.

Lewis, Brig. Sir Clinton, O.B.E., and Col. J. D. Campbell, D.S.O., eds. *Oxford American Atlas.* New York: Oxford University Press, 1951.

Manker, Ernst. *People of Eight Seasons: The History of the Lapps.* New York: Viking Press, 1963.

Martin, Anthony. *Norwegian Life and Landscape.* Elel Books, 1985.

Moore, Capt. A. R. *Careless Word . . . A Needless Sinking,* rev. ed. Kings Point, NY: Merchant Marine Museum, 1984.

Morison, Samuel E. *History of U.S. Naval Operations in World War II.* Boston: Little Brown & Co., 1947.

Palmer, M. B. *We Fight with Merchant Ships.* Indianapolis: Bobbs-Merrill Co., 1943.

Pemsel, Helmut. *A History of War at Sea: An Atlas and Chronology of Conflict at Sea.* Translated by Maj. G. D. G. Smith. Annapolis: Naval Institute Press, 1977.

Petrow, Richard. *The Bitter Years: The Invasion and Occupation of Denmark and Norway, 1940–1945.* London: P. B. S., 1974.

Pitt, Barrie. *World War II: The Battle of the Atlantic.* New York: Time-Life Books, 1986.

Schofield, William G. *Eastward the Convoys.* Skokie, Ill.: Rand McNally & Co., 1965.

Smith, O. M. Interviews with T. E. Simmons. Taped August, 1988, to August, 1989.

Sulzberger, C. L., and the editors of *American Heritage Magazine of History. The American Heritage Picture History of World War II.* Boston: Houghton Mifflin, 1987.

Ulam, Adam B. *Stalin: The Man and His Era.* New York: Viking Press, 1973.

Vanberg, Bent. *Of Norwegian Ways.* New York: Barnes & Noble, 1970.

Villiers, Capt. Alan. *Men, Ships, and the Sea.* Washington, D.C.: National Geographic Society, 1962.